LIFE AFTER
BAGHDAD

In memory of two great Egyptian friends

NAGUIB MAHFOUZ
(1911–2006)

and

HUSAYN FAWZI
(1900–1988)

true humanists who never gave up hope

LIFE AFTER BAGHDAD

Memoirs of an Arab-Jew in Israel, 1950–2000

SASSON SOMEKH

Translated by Tamar L. Cohen

sussex
ACADEMIC
PRESS
Brighton • Portland • Toronto

2 4 6 8 10 9 7 5 3 1

First published in 2012 by
SUSSEX ACADEMIC PRESS
PO Box 139
Eastbourne BN24 9BP

and in the United States of America by
SUSSEX ACADEMIC PRESS
920 NE 58th Ave   Suite 300
Portland, Oregon 97213-3786

and in Canada by
SUSSEX ACADEMIC PRESS (CANADA)
8000 Bathurst Street, Unit 1, PO Box 30010, Vaughan, Ontario L4J 0C6

British Library Cataloguing in Publication Data
A CIP catalogue record for this book is available from the British Library.

Library of Congress Cataloging-in-Publication Data
Somekh, Sasson.
Life after Baghdad : memoirs of an Arab-Jew in Israel, 1950–2000 / Sasson
  Somekh.
p. cm.
Includes bibliographical references and index.
ISBN 978-1-84519-502-1 (p/b : alk. paper)   1. Somekh, Sasson. 2. Jews,
Iraqi—Israel—Biography. 3. College teachers—Israel—Biography.
4. Arabic teachers—Israel—Biography. I. Title.
DS113.8.I72S66 2012
956.9405092—dc23
  [B]

2011040267

Typeset and designed by Sussex Academic Press, Brighton & Eastbourne.
Printed by TJ International, Padstow, Cornwall.
This book is printed on acid-free paper.

CONTENTS

LIST OF ILLUSTRATIONS

The illustrations are placed after page 162.

1 With Naguib Mahfouz in his latter years, Cairo, 2004.
2 The author with his family, Ramat Gan, Israel, 1996.
3 Avigal, the author's daughter, with Naguib Mahfouz at the novelist's residence, Cairo, 1982.
4 Professsor Haim Blanc listening to recordings of Arabic dialects, *c.* 1960.
5 Professor S. D. Goitein, *c.* 1980.
6 Dr. Mustafa Badawi at his office, Pusey Lane, Oxford, *c.* 1990.
7 Dr. Husayn Fawzi with Terrie Somekh, Paris, 1980.
8 With Egyptian writer Naim Takla (right) and Israeli writer Aharon Amir (left), Alexandria, 1990.
9 With Egyptian playwright Ali Salem at the Israeli Academic Center, Cairo, 1996.
10 With Naguib Mahfouz at Champs Elysees Café, Alexandria, 1982.
11 With Professor Edward Said, Stockholm, 1993.
12 With Mrs. Shulamit Aloni, former Israeli minister of education and Professor Ali Atiyya, professor of Hebrew literature at Eyn Shams University, Cairo. Photo taken in Tel Aviv, *c.* 1997.
13 At the Israeli Academic Center in Cairo during a lecture by Israeli novelist Sami Michael (third from left), 1995.

PREFACE

This book is the second volume of my memoirs, following *Baghdad, Yesterday* (English version, Ibis Editions, Jerusalem 2007). That book consisted of memories from the days of my childhood and youth in the Iraqi capital, the city of my birth, up until my departure for Israel in 1951. The places and times of the present volume are different. Today, Baghdad is a place that I cannot visit, as much as I would like to, for reasons well-known. Tel Aviv, Jerusalem, Oxford, Princeton, and Cairo are the geographical background of the present book, which spans the years from the mid-point of the twentieth century to the beginning of the twenty-first. A half century was spent engaged in the study and teaching of modern Arabic literature at many universities, many far away from one another. In Tel Aviv, the city that today I call home, Arabic is not my primary language of speech or writing, but thanks to my research and to my students, some of whom are native Arabic speakers, I have kept in touch with my mother tongue, and my connection to Arabic literature has never faded.

I intended to use these chapters in order to recount my life and my many years of professional activity, but no less than that, it was my desire to describe people who are dear to me and who appeared in my life at different places and times during the past fifty years. To six of these friends I have devoted entire chapters: the Egyptian scientist and author Husayn Fawzi, the Jerusalemite linguist Haim Blanc, the great Genizah scholar Shlomo Dov Goitein, the Israeli poet Alexander Penn, my advisor at Oxford University, Dr. Mustafa Badawi, and, last but not least, Nobel Prize for literature laureate, Naguib Mahfouz, to whom I devote the longest chapter in this book.

The Hebrew edition of the book was published in Tel Aviv in 2008, and as I prepare its English version, the Arab east is going through days of change. Egypt, the country to which I became so personally attached, is now experiencing a trying time, which all those who love her hope will lead to a safe shore. I do not wish to conjecture about how things will turn out, and indeed, throughout my life as an educator I have advised my students to stay away from prediction; they have enough work awaiting them in understanding the past and the present.

I confess that many of my experiences over the past fifty years could not find a place in this book, and I at no point considered cramming into it all of the things I have experienced and the personalities who have crossed my path in Israel and abroad. I have preferred, in this portrait of my life and my surroundings, to convey the essence and not the detail, to present the highlights and not engage in pedantry or flowery description.

Many times I felt the urge to go into the minutiae of my research and the obstacles I encountered on occasion in the research process. But on second thought I have not allowed myself get carried away, lest I bore my future reader. My wife Terrie, who read through the entire manuscript before it was submitted to the press, also advised me in many cases to omit passages that were too "technical" or which related to people or places that would have no relevance for the English reader, and I am grateful for her insights. I would also like to thank my translator Tamar Cohen for her efforts to give the English version its present form. Two friends who read parts of the manuscript also deserve my appreciation: Peter Theroux and Judith Roumani.

CHAPTER
1
THE TRANSIT CAMP

I arrived on my own from Baghdad in Israel in March 1951, three months prior to my parents. A feeling of elation, of absolute freedom, came over me as I stepped off the direct flight from Baghdad to Lydda airport near Tel Aviv; but I also felt a weight of responsibility as I had never felt before. What would I do now? Where would I turn? I hadn't the slightest idea. The following day I traveled to Jerusalem to look into enrolling in the Hebrew University. While in the capital I met a few friends who had arrived in Israel before me. Some were studying in the Arabic Department and others had registered in the Faculty of Sciences (in chemistry or biology, for example). I returned somewhat heartened, although I did not have in hand my diploma from the Shammash High School in Baghdad, and would have to await the arrival of the documents my parents were trying to "smuggle" to me.

Two weeks in the Sha'ar Ha-Aliyah transit camp near Haifa. I observed the colorful stream of people arriving on the Baghdad–Lydda flights. I was not familiar with all of the social classes comprising the Baghdad Jewish community, not to mention the Jews of northern Iraq – Kurds, and those from Mosul and its environs. I went to Tel Aviv to visit my uncle – my mother's brother, Fred, who lived with his family on Balfour Street in "Little Tel Aviv" (the adjacent Allenby Street was the city's main artery at the time). It was reassuring to be greeted by relatives, open-armed and ready to help with anything; yet I was not looking for a "sponsor" or a "patron", and was therefore determined to return to the camp and make my way.

I returned to Sha'ar Ha-Aliyah with some cash in my pocket, enough to get me through the coming weeks. Riding the bus, I gazed out for the first time at the scenery of my new country and took in the smells of the orchards that were then still scattered along the coastal plain. The intoxicating citrus fragrance heightened the feeling of anticipation that had begun to fill me. At twilight, the bus from Tel Aviv dropped me off next to Sha'ar Ha-Aliyah. From within the camp I heard a tune, a melancholy Iraqi voice crooning about the travails of love and fate. And then all the difficult sights returned: Families. Hundreds, maybe thousands of families in all sorts of dress – some in suits and winter coats and others in summer clothes, a pandemonium of colors and styles; children scurrying around the huts and tents that housed their families, and adult vociferations that attested from afar to the discomfort and the upheaval these people had gone through. But beyond the words, which I could not quite make out as I neared the camp, I could clearly detect the anxiety that seized these new inhabitants of the State of Israel: What would be? What future awaited them and their children? What about their studies and jobs that were cut off so suddenly? Where would they live and what would they do? The present was stifling. Most of these families were used to living in brick buildings, between solid walls. Here they were greeted by rickety canvas huts (which came to be known as "badonim" – from the Hebrew word *badd* or "canvas"), with makeshift, cracked floors. All day long, from right and left, the voices of the tenants of these canvas huts could be heard: Where were their neighbors of yesterday? When would they arrive? And if they had already arrived: where would they be dispatched by the Jewish Agency clerks, who themselves knew little about future settlement and employment prospects? Immigrants waited on long lines three times a day for their food; there was no shopping to be found in the vicinity. An attempt to see a doctor or a nurse entailed more waiting, followed by the language barrier between them and those who treated them. Their complaints to the "absorption" agents were met with a standard answer: "Look, we're doing our best. The work is hard for us, too. And this is just a transition period. In a few days you'll be living in another place, something more permanent, and you'll be able to build normal lives for yourselves. So stop whining and complaining."

But the grievances and discomfort began to gnaw at these otherwise joyful people, and at the expectations they had had of moving to their own country, where no one would be able to humiliate them because of their religion. Bitterness now began to spread. The fact that the Jewish Agency clerks spoke Yiddish among themselves (they, too, were new immigrants – Holocaust survivors who had arrived from Eastern Europe not long before), created a feeling, for the first time among many of the Iraqis, that they were second-class citizens, that only a Yiddish speaker could aspire to the status of a full-fledged citizen.

Another, separate, problem arose a short time after the beginning of the arrival of the Iraqi Jews: a loosening of the social order and crumbling of the firm class structure that had characterized their lives until then. The middle, clerical, class, was annoyed that members of the lower class ("the servant class", as it were) now felt free to act like bosses in the Iraqi Jewish community. Now that the residents of the various Baghdadi neighborhoods had begun to mingle, the inhabitants of the dilapidated apartments of north Baghdad could brag about the palaces they had ostensibly left behind. To add insult to injury, love stories between young people from different classes became common, since there were now no geographical or economic divisions between them. It was difficult for the parents of a young person from the middle class to accept the fact that their son or daughter wanted to marry into a family from the working class, or even worse, of servants. A twenty-year-old man I knew, who had fallen in love back in Baghdad with the daughter of his family's maid, took advantage of the new situation to marry his beloved, since his parents could no longer control his life (they did indeed marry, and the couple's children grew up and prospered in Israel. As far as I recall, one of their children became an influential attorney).

And even more than these marriages of "unequals" within the Iraqi community, even greater distress and anger was caused by the "mixed marriages" that were becoming increasingly common: groups of immigrants from Romania were arriving in those same days, and friendships and romantic relationships developed among the young neighbors from two different worlds. In most cases it would be an Iraqi young man with a Romanian young woman, since Iraqi girls were not yet allowed the freedom of unsupervised movement and association that their brothers had begun to have in Israel. As for the young men – friendship or an "affair" with a Romanian girl was an

unexpected triumph. The Romanian girls were "European", sometimes with "European beauty" and "European manners"; in other
words, the Romanian girls in those days were freer than the Iraqi girls
in their relations with the opposite sex, or as the young people put
it: "Romanian girls are easier".

On occasion, such contact between Iraqi boys and Romanian girls
resulted in marriage. The families of the young men saw such a
wedding as an "abduction", and even as the marriage of an honest
man with a "loose woman" – all this because they were afraid that
their sons were attracted to these girls because they were apparently
ready to have "sinful relations" before being lawfully wed. Thus,
instead of a *farah* – a joyful wedding – the occasion would take place
in a heavy atmosphere, and sometimes even without the participation
of the groom's parents.

Another source of distress for the temporary inhabitants of Sha'ar
Ha-Aliyah came from an unexpected place. Some of the Iraqi immigrants had sent the remains of their money at the last moment via
illicit money agents, and occasionally one could hear cries of horror
from within the hut of a family that had just found out that their
money agent, who had given them the name of his "representative"
in Israel, had embezzled their money and that the so-called representative did not even exist. One family I knew wept bitterly when
their small fortune was stolen in such a way. They had owned a small
house near ours in Baghdad, which they managed to sell just a day or
two before the Iraqi parliament suddenly passed a law freezing all the
assets of Jews who had registered for renunciation of nationality.
Overjoyed, they thanked God for their good fortune. But now, when
they came to receive the funds that would take them out of their
misery and into prosperity, they found themselves completely at a
loss. And thus they turned overnight from members of the middle
class to paupers.

Despite all of these troubles and upheavals, whose severity I did
not make light of, I nonetheless felt a sense of relief on the familial
and political horizon, and clung to the hope in my heart regarding
the future. There I was, defending Israel, as it were, and trying to
convince the grumblers that the situation wasn't so bad: What did
you expect when you decided to gamble and give up your Iraqi citi-
zenship? That you'd walk right into a palace or villa on the seashore?
That you'd learn Hebrew during the two-hour flight? That you'd be

given a house comparable to the one you had abroad, in a neighborhood charted out according to the old Baghdad neighborhoods?
Every time I set out to assuage the great frustration that came out of
the mouths of these Jews, I would regret having to defend a regime
that was not in principle to my liking, being a socialist myself.
Moreover, I felt that I was being unforgivably selfish. For me, things
were good and comfortable in this place and time, and the intoxicating aroma of citrus clouded my judgment when it came to the
hardship of my fellow immigrants. From my selfish perspective, in
any case, I do not remember any negative things about Sha'ar Ha-
Aliyah (where I spent only two or three weeks, all in all), except for
the endless lines, including the line for meals at the end of which we
were served food that was not to our liking (one item, the herring,
was served ad nauseum). The egg-powder omelet – one of the staples
of the strict rationing that was practiced in those years – was like an
otherworldly punishment. But the worst thing of all to bear was the
humiliation of having to stand in a long line with others, waiting for
food to be dished out. We couldn't help but compare this experience
to a soup kitchen or, even worse, to the feeding of dogs at a kennel.

In the final chapter of my book *Baghdad, Yesterday*, I dedicated a few
paragraphs to the linguistic problems encountered by the Iraqi immigrants in Israel, and I think it is worthwhile to address this issue
again:

The Jews of Iraq did not arrive knowing Hebrew, certainly not the
kind of Hebrew that had developed in Israel. Those who had studied
in Jewish schools, in particular in religious schools, learned a Hebrew
that was "Iraqi" in pronunciation and pre-modern in its linguistics.
The meanings of words were not always identical to those existing in
Israel, not to mention the different accent. While the pronunciation
of the vowels was not significantly different (in contrast to the
Yiddish-inflected Hebrew, which had a distinct pronunciation of
most of the vowels from Israeli Hebrew), the consonants were quite
different. First of all, the Iraqi Jews pronounced the guttural consonants such as Het, Tet, 'Ayin, and Qof; in the "native" Israeli (or
"Sabra") accent, the guttural 'Ayin was swallowed up in a soft Aleph,
which was sometimes indistinguishable from the consonant Heh,

making it all the more difficult for Iraqis to understand the Hebrew spoken by a "Sabra". A similar thing happened with the consonant Het, which was swallowed into the Khaf, while the general disappearance of the consonants Tet and Qof in the Israeli accent (even among the minority in Israel that did pronounce the guttural Het and 'Ayin) became an object of ridicule in the eyes of Iraqi immigrants. How did the word Catastrophe become Qatastrophe? For the Iraqi newcomers, these were not only differences in pronunciation, but veritable distortions that impeded their understanding of important words in the contemporary language. Words that should have been easy for speakers of one Semitic language to understand in another Semitic language were incomprehensible for them; a situation whereby a speaker of Yiddish or Polish could more easily deal with thousands of words in the new language.

Ultimately, not only was the Hebrew some of the Iraqi immigrants brought with them to Israel not useful for communication; it turned out to be a burden. Thus the outcry against the abandonment of the guttural in standard Israeli Hebrew was not merely a linguistic-"ideological" dispute, trying to preserve one kind of speech over another along the East West pronunciation (and demographic) divide. Above all, the complaint was against the impediments it caused to the comprehension of "native" Israeli Hebrew by those with a Middle Eastern accent (not to mention the fact that the Middle Eastern accent was oftentimes a subject of mockery and parody for veteran Israelis because it was reminiscent of Arabic). For myself and my peers, who arrived without any knowledge of Hebrew, things were easier. We learned Hebrew in a different setting. In the army, where we were drafted a short time after our arrival, we could imitate the Israeli-born soldiers of Ashkenazi (or mixed) origin, and adopt for ourselves the non-Middle Eastern accent. Eventually, when, around 1960, I became a member of the secretariat of the Academy of Hebrew Language and I had spokesperson responsibilities, it was to my advantage that I could pronounce the guttural Het and 'Ayin, but it took some time for me to get used to doing so naturally and without hyper-correction.

CHAPTER

2

LOOKING AROUND

Not once during my youth in Baghdad did I experience the pleasure of a group trip. In those years, the Jews – and specifically the Jewish schools – avoided making annual or seasonal excursions, due to the aftershocks of the "Farhud" of 1941, and even more so after the adoption of the UN Partition Plan for Palestine in 1947. He who values his life, they said, should stay safely at home and avoid group activities that might make him stand out.

Students from older grades would tell us about the trips they had taken, accompanied by their teachers, to the ancient historical sites in the center and south of Iraq, of which there were many: the statue of the lion of ancient Babylonia, the minaret at Samarra, etc. We listened to their stories with jealousy and wonder. I do recall from my early childhood, however, the Saturday family picnics we took near our house at Al-Sa'adoun Park, which was modeled after London's Hyde Park; and of course – the summer evenings spent on the small islands that appeared in the middle of the Tigris River when the tide ebbed, about which I wrote in *Baghdad, Yesterday*.

In Israel, things were different. Not two or three weeks had passed from the day I arrived there, in March 1951, when I got my first taste of a group trip across this small country. At first, such excursions took place under the auspices of the youth movements or as part of the activities of the youth branches of the Zionist parties, such as Ha-Mahanot Ha-Olim (The Labor Party Youth Movement) or Ha-Shomer Ha-Tza'ir (The Socialist Zionist Youth Movement); later on I partook of such trips during my intensive Hebrew language course (*ulpan*) at the Hadassim Youth Village; and finally, in the army and in the Young Communist League. I loved these outings, which I had so longed for in the past. The moment I heard that a trip was to take place, I would sign up. I was enthralled by the expanses of the

Jezreel Valley, the Sea of Galilee, the Kibbutzim in the Galilee, as well as Nazareth and the Arab villages in the area. To this day, I have a warm spot in my heart for the Jezreel Valley, ever since I overlooked the valley from the hills and watched the breezes leisurely tousling the great rectangular green plains. Then there were the songs sung (mostly by the members of the youth movements) on the way from one stop to another. I remember one song in particular, which was based on the symphonic poem by composer Mark Lavri called "Emeq" (Valley), and which opens with the following words:

Blue steel is the sky
A red furnace is my heart
Today I'll burn the remains of the night
With the flames of my sorrow.

And continues:
Light, light
All the valley is drunk
The Gilboa is kissing the Tabor

I got to know Nazareth and the surrounding villages in a different way, namely, on individual outings. I had passed through Nazareth on one of the group trips, at which time I discovered an Arab bookshop. Very eager to find books in my mother tongue, I delayed the van's return. Later, one of the counselors chastised me (gently, I must add) in the following words: "What are you reading Arabic for? That is the language of your exile. You must get used to reading books in Hebrew." Looking back, I am impressed by the fact that she did not describe my mother tongue, Arabic, as "my enemy's language". Had she only known how much I loved the "language of my exile", and how I had already begun to fall deeply in love with the new-old language, Hebrew, whose proximity to Arabic made it all the more appealing to me.

From that day on I began to make occasional visits to Nazareth and the nearby villages; since the aforementioned bookstore (which was, if I am not mistaken, the only one in the city) did not possess the books I was looking for, I turned to the rich private libraries of the city's intellectuals, and thus met several Arab writers and poets, with whom I developed long-lasting friendships. Among them were the poets Jamal Qa'war, Michel Haddad, and Tawfiq Zayyad (who would later become the beloved mayor of the city). I fell madly in love with the Sea of Galilee and its historic and modern shores. Since I had already mastered the art of swimming in the Tigris, I enjoyed swimming far out in the Sea of Galilee on my own. Sometimes, in the middle of a relaxing swim, a lifeguard would come by in a noisy motorboat and scold me for having dared to stray so far from the designated swimming area.

But when it came to the Israeli Arabs I met – those same Palestinians who had remained in their towns and villages (a little over one hundred thousand in all) after most of the indigenous population had fled their lands – with these I forged relationships in various, sometimes surprising, ways. As a matter of fact, the first Israeli person I met was none other than the writer Emile Habiby, a Christian Arab. This incident deserves a digression since it was saturated with fate and coincidence.

The story is as follows: upon my arrival at Sha'ar Ha-Aliyah, as I related in the previous chapter, I felt somewhat suffocated. The camp was surrounded by barbed wire and the new immigrants were warned against wandering outside of the camp, lest they get lost. As an unbridled youth of seventeen who had only just now discovered the meaning of absolute freedom (my parents, the reader will recall, were still in Iraq, and I was to be, for three months, the sole master of my fate), I decided to try to reach Haifa on foot, about a half hour's distance at a brisk pace. As I came upon the outer streets of the city, I came upon a different urban reality than what I had expected. It did not have the feel of a new, "pioneering", settlement. Rather, it was an Arab neighborhood called Wadi Nisnas, whose narrow streets reminded me in certain places of the commercial area of Baghdad. Upon entering the neighborhood, I noticed that the walls were plastered with posters about the upcoming parliamentary elections for the second Knesset. The large poster that was pasted on almost every wall said in Arabic "Vote 'Qof' and do not fear" – The letter "Qof" referred to the Israeli Communist Party, otherwise known as "Maki". These posters truly amazed me. Although I had known that there was a communist party that participated in the elections in Israel, and that it already had representatives in the first Knesset, these Arabic posters filled my heart with joy. After all, in my home country, not only was the Left forbidden from operating openly, but the leaders of

9

the Party – of various ethnicities, including Jews – were sometimes even hung in public simply for being communists. Not only was it unthinkable to see a communist-party campaign poster displayed in Baghdad, but a pedestrian captured carrying a copy of the party's underground newspaper, *al-Qa`ida*, in his pocket, could be put on trial and given an extended prison sentence. And here I was, seeing with my own eyes – in Israel, the state of the Jews – giant posters in the language of their ostensible enemies, campaigning for the Communist list, whose second and fourth candidates were Palestinian Arabs. My enthusiasm for the Israeli democratic system eventually abated once I stopped seeing the tyrannical Iraqi regime as an object of comparison; and when, over the years, I saw the degree of democracy practiced in Europe (Italy, France, England), I stopped being so impressed by what I found in Israel.

Walking along Khoury Street, the main street of the "Wadi", I came upon a small building with a large sign reading *Al-Ittihad*. That was the name of the Israeli Communist Party's Arabic-language weekly, which had been published in the past by the Palestinian Arab Communist Organization of which Emile Habiby was a leader. In 1949 they united with the Jewish Communist Organization to form Maki. In my youth in Baghdad I used to linger beside the newsstand at the entrance to the Banks Street (where my father worked) and look at the newspapers coming from the Arab world (and sometimes from Europe). Among these, I was drawn to the editions of *Al-Ittihad* that arrived from Palestine, but, knowing that it was a "dangerous" newspaper, I did not dare buy it or even come near enough to read the headlines. Here I was, actually standing opposite the office of this newspaper, so how could I not go in and try and speak with its staff? I walked in, somewhat hesitant, and to my great surprise I was greeted, by chance, by none other than Emile Habiby, the newspaper's editor. He was about thirty years old at the time, but his name preceded him, thanks to his positive role in uniting the Jewish and Arab branches of the Communist Party and because of his weekly political column in *Al-Ittihad*, which he signed "Juhayna" (that was the name of Emile's eldest daughter, whom I would meet later on, on one of my visits to his home in Nazareth).

I told Emile what I knew about the situation in Iraq. Since I had no connection with the Iraqi Communist Party, and therefore no "insider" information to pass on, I made do with literary matters, such as the rise of the new poetic form known as "free verse" in the Baghdad coffee shops. Emile had little interest in modern poetry, but he could recite many Arabic poems from the golden age of medieval Arabic literature. For his part, he spoke to me of the tragedy that had befallen the Palestinian Arabs, about the grim fate of the hundreds of thousands of refugees and also about the difficult personal and cultural reality faced by those who remained in the State of Israel (despite the fact that, aside from those who were considered "present absentees", the Arabs were now considered citizens like the rest of the inhabitants of Israel). I knew these facts in a general sense, but the concrete details Habiby laid out before me filled me with concern. In my visits to the Arab villages in the Galilee over the following weeks, I saw with my own eyes the full truth of his assertions. Most of the residents of these villages, generally farmers, were distressed by the fact that the Israeli government was intending to dispossess many of the Arab villages of their agricultural lands, using false claims and making sure to erase the traces of the abandoned villages and register the lands as "without owners".

In that same first meeting in Wadi Nisnas, Emile Habiby tried to persuade me to take an active part in his party's campaign. He expected an "enlightened" person like myself to help the party make its voice heard among the masses of immigrants who were arriving daily from Iraq and from other countries. My response was something like this: "Give me a break, I just arrived in the country yesterday. How am I supposed to get involved in a campaign before I've even seen what the country looks like?" The truth is that this was my way of avoiding giving an affirmative answer. I was still not convinced that the Israeli Communist Party was the right "home" for me, and despite my leftist views, I was inclined in those days toward Mapam (The United Workers' Party), in particular to its left wing. Admittedly, at the beginning of my time in Israel, I was more attracted to this latter party and its associated kibbutzim of the Shomer Ha-Tza'ir youth movement, than to the Arab villages scattered throughout the Galilee. Among other things, this was because kibbutz society as a social and ecological model was unlike anything I had ever known, and certainly different from the Arab villages in Israel. Kibbutzim like Merhavia and Mishmar Ha-Emeq captured my imagination because they were "egalitarian" communes; indeed, the Left around the world (including Iraq) was enamored of kibbutz

ʒy. This enthusiasm was succeeded by an equally powerful disil-
ɔnment as the human, economic, and ideological difficulties
ɹerged from the kibbutzim in the coming decades. What already
ʋisturbed me back then in Mapam and its kibbutzim was the fact
that membership in the party was limited to Jewish citizens. Arab
supporters of the party were organized in a separate unit, and Arab
youngsters who wanted to experience kibbutz life could only stay for
extended visits and were put in a separate framework known, if I
recall correctly, as "the organization of Arab Pioneering Youth".

In contradistinction to this, Maki was a bi-national party in the
full sense of the word. Arab and Jewish members participated in its
leadership and its assemblies without discrimination, and its representatives in the Knesset and in the Israel Labor Federation included
both Jews and Arabs. In general, Arab representatives were field
activists or involved in a professional union, although the Arab
membership also had its intellectuals. Emile Habiby himself, the
intellectual of the party's northern branch, was also the man-in-the-
field for that region. He was a charismatic speaker preparing for
membership in the second Knesset, which was about to be elected.
There were four or five more Arab intellectuals among the party's
activists, whom I met soon after my arrival in Israel and who accompanied Maki until the 1970s. The first was Emile Tuma, a historian
and ideologue who at the time of the discussions of the Partition Plan
was one of those who opposed the Soviet position in support of the
partition; in time, however, he returned to the fold of the bi-national
party and participated in it as a full member. The second was Saliba
Khamis, a Nazarene who for a while was also head of the city's party
branch. He was editor of some of the party's publications, and in the
1990s distanced himself from Rakah (an offshoot of Maki) due to
ideological disagreements. The third, Jabra Nicola, a resident of
Haifa and a veteran Palestinian journalist, was one of the editors of
Al-Ittihad (later on appointed editor of *Al-Jadid*, the literary monthly
of the party, to which I contributed on occasion). There was always a
certain tension between Jabra and the party's leadership, which
apparently resulted from Jabra's Trotskyite inclinations and in the
intellectual haughtiness he demonstrated toward many of his fellow
members. And last but not least, Hanna Abu-Hanna, from the village
of Reineh next to Nazareth, a poet and teacher, who in the 1950s and
60s was one of the heads of the Young Communist League. He later

returned to the world of education to direct the prestigious Arabic Orthodox High School in Haifa. All four of the intellectuals mentioned were Christians, born into various Christian denominations (of Emile Habiby and Hanna Abu-Hanna, at least, I know that they were born into the Anglican Church, to which only a minority of Palestinian Christians belong). The first three died in the eighties and nineties, while Hanna Abu-Hanna is alive and still working at the time of the writing of these lines (2011) in Haifa, where he has lived and written since the 1970s.

And what of the Muslim intellectuals? Many of the Muslim intellectuals who remained in Israel had a traditional education, having studied in religious schools. It is therefore not surprising that several of the Muslims who assumed leadership in Israel came from the field of law, and numbered among the judges in the Shari'a courts. Others became integrated into the general court system in Israel, and, in the 1990s, one Muslim judge reached a seat on the Israel Supreme Court. There were only a few Muslims among the central Maki activists, the most prominent among them being Tawfiq Zayyad, who became mayor of Nazareth after serving as party head in the city and its environs. I became friendly with Zayyad in my first years in Israel, when he saw himself as a young proletarian poet, and in due course I even translated some of his poems into Hebrew. My last meeting with him took place around 1990. He was mayor of Nazareth at the time, and I went to his office at City Hall to ask him to pay tribute to my friend, the veteran Nazarene poet Michel Haddad (1919-1996), by granting him the municipal support that would allow him to publish all his poems in a single volume. Zayyad's response surprised me in its firmness. He reminded me of the harsh past disagreements between Maki and Haddad, who had been accused of being a "collaborator" with the Israeli government. I told him that it seemed to me that as mayor he could let bygones be bygones and focus on the fact that Haddad was the devoted bard of modern Nazareth, at least in my opinion. My mission failed in this case. But for the most part Zayyad was a convivial person, full of *joie de vivre*. He died tragically in a car accident while returning from a party with friends in the West Bank.

CHAPTER
3

THE TIGRIS
AND THE JORDAN

The rest of my family – my parents, sister, and brother – arrived in Israel on a flight from Baghdad in mid-June 1951, some three months after I did. During my time alone I had traveled throughout the country and began to know it and its inhabitants. I rushed to Lydda airport (today Ben-Gurion Airport) to greet them, as I had been notified of the time of their arrival by some newcomers who had flown in two or three days earlier. A great joy came over me as I watched them descend from the plane, even if it signified the end of the absolute freedom I had enjoyed in those few months. The passengers, my family included, looked somewhat ridiculous. They wore their finest clothing – heavy clothes in the heat of summer – so as not to squander the little room they had in the small number of suitcases allotted them. My father, whom I had never seen wearing anything on his head, donned a new English wool hat (which he would never use in Israel; it would remain in the closet). My younger brother (thirteen years old) wore a straw-brimmed hat that my parents had purchased after hearing about the brutal Israeli sun. As for my mother, she wore her heavy fur coat.

The registration and naturalization process was quick (by then they had stopped spraying the immigrants with DDT). The accommodations had changed in the meanwhile, that is, since I had arrived in March, and immigrants were no longer brought to a temporary transit camp (Sha'ar Ha-Aliyah, in my case) before being sent to a permanent transit camp (indeed transit camps became the permanent residence of many of the newcomers, despite the oxymoron "permanent transit"). Thus, the new arrivals were ordered, along with their

14

luggage, onto a pick-up truck, to be taken to a new transit camp that had just been established in Ra'anana, about twenty minutes from Tel Aviv. I got on the truck with them, and to my family's great surprise, when the truck driver got lost on the short trip from Lydda to Ra'anana, it was I who put him back on track. My parents were impressed by the Hebrew I spoke with the driver, since they did not know Hebrew and my broken speech sounded in their ears like the pinnacle of fluency in the language of their forefathers.

We were dropped off in Ra'anana at nightfall, in an old, temporary residential area a short way from the new transit camp that the Jewish Agency had used until then as a holding area, and from which we were supposed to walk in the sand to the new site. The residents, themselves recent arrivals, approached and advised us not to walk to the new camp. The people there would be put in dilapidated tents, they said, and what was worse: that area was full of scorpions and snakes. A few helpful souls suggested to my parents that they take their suitcases to an unoccupied wooden shack (which had once been a public bath) where they could spend the night and think the whole matter over at their leisure the following day. We did as they advised and ended up spending the following three or four months in this shack, until we purchased a small apartment in a public housing project in Bat Yam, into which we moved before the winter. Our small temporary "home" in Ra'anana was not lacking in problems; more specifically, it had all sorts of blood-sucking fleas that lived in the mattresses and had free reign at night. We took great pains to drag the five heavy mattresses outside each morning and lay them in the sun for a few hours, but these efforts were in vain. My mother bore most of the burden, since my father, sister, and I headed out toward Tel Aviv each day to seek out our fortune! My brother Henry-Aharon was taken in for a few months at Kibbutz Hatzor next to Gedera, between Tel Aviv and Beer Sheva, where cousins of ours had just been accepted as members. At least he was spared the horrors of the bloodthirsty fleas.

For weeks, and in fact throughout our entire stay in Ra'anana, none of us found work. My father would meet old friends on Tel Aviv's Rothschild Avenue, next to the banking district, and would return home with stories of what had become of Baghdadi immigrants whom he knew or knew of. Soon enough, both my father and I were accepted into intensive Hebrew language courses, and for several weeks we boarded at our respective Ulpans, leaving my mother and sister alone in the shack.

The language barrier was the greatest challenge to my parents' acclimatization to Israel. It took many months for them to be able to hold any sort of conversation with anyone who did not speak Arabic or English, in other words, with the established Jewish residents of the country. At the end of weeks of intensive Hebrew study, my father, 51 years old, had not gone from a state of ignorance to one of mastery of the language. On the contrary, he remained – perhaps until the day he died five years later – never having really learned Hebrew. I look now at a small picture of his class, which was held in one of the settlements in the Sharon region, not far from Netanya, and my heart aches as I compare my Ulpan at Hadassim to the shabby building where my father's Ulpan was held. In the picture, his eyes betray worry, difficulty, and above all – a certain awkwardness that I had never seen in him in Baghdad.

I could write at length about my Hebrew studies, but I will try here to recount the events in brief. I was determined to devote myself to the study of Hebrew language and literature, and of course to attain full fluency in spoken Hebrew. I heard that some people I knew had been accepted into an intensive Ulpan for immigrant teachers at the Hadassim Youth Village, located between Ra'anana and Netanya. I mailed in a request and received a response that the opening date had not yet been set. I waited patiently for about two months, and finally wrote a letter, the first I ever wrote in Hebrew, to the editor of *Omer*, the simplified and vocalized[1] daily supplementary for new immigrants of *Davar*, the Labor party daily. Thirty years later, to my surprise, I found my letter, alongside the newspaper's response, reproduced in Mordechai Naor's book *Immigrants and Transit Camps 1948–1952* (Jerusalem 1984), and I take the liberty to include the text of the letter here in its entirety:

> Two months ago I read a notice in the newspaper about courses for teachers that the Ministry of Education and Culture is organizing. I submitted a request and received a response on May 30 that it had been decided to accept me and that I would receive a notice about

1 Vocalization in Hebrew is the addition of vowel signs above and below the letters to make the reading unambiguous.

the venue of the Ulpan and its opening date. More than a month has passed and I have not yet received a letter. What should I do?

Two days later came a response from the Ministry of Education, which was summarized by the editor of *Omer* as follows:

A few days ago we published a letter from Sasson Somekh in *Omer*, saying that on the 30th of May he received a notice that he had been accepted to an Ulpan and that since then he has been waiting for another notice as to when he should come to the Ulpan to begin his studies.

The Ministry of Education and Culture has just notified us that on June 27 it sent Sasson Somekh a letter informing him that he was accepted to the Hadassim Ulpan and that the Ulpan will open on July 8. The Ministry of Education assumes that the letter got lost in the mail.

I was overjoyed to receive this answer, and I was proud that my letter to the editor had been published without corrections and that it had gotten such a prompt answer.

I spent three wonderful months at Hadassim. I was a young man, not yet eighteen years old, while most of the men and women who were accepted along with me to the Ulpan were experienced teachers (all of them newcomers from Iraq). They ranged in age from thirty to fifty, and like my father, they had trouble catching on to Hebrew. The short, intensive Ulpan was aimed at teaching Hebrew to experienced new-immigrant teachers so that they could quickly find work as teachers (in elementary schools, for the most part) in the transit camps and new settlements. For this purpose, the directors of the Ulpan made sure, besides teaching language and grammar, to provide a curriculum that was rich with subjects and activities: local geography (commonly known as "knowledge of the land"), lessons in local flora and fauna, Israeli history, songs, and chapters from the Hebrew Bible. The teachers who taught us these subjects belonged to the parent-institution, Hadassim, and most of them were dedicated, energetic educators. I remember one teacher named Ze'ev, whose descriptions of nature and the lay of the land fascinated me. He told us in great detail about the Jordan River and its vegetation. When we finally went on a hike by the Jordan River itself I suffered a great disappointment. I had imagined the Jordan as a river to be reckoned with (like the biblical "thicket of the Jordan"), as broad as the Tigris from my native city, or maybe a little bit narrower. But what I saw was a small stream, almost without flowing water (it was summertime). I challenged the teacher: what about all that talk in the Bible about crossing the Jordan? And what about the bridges that were built over it and the waterworks we talked about in class? A little embarrassed, Ze'ev went on to speak about the neglect of the shores of the river over the generations.

I enjoyed every one of the subjects I studied at Hadassim, all of which made me want to know more about the history and nature of Israel, but I never forgot my "sacred" goal: to learn Hebrew, and to learn it well. I remember days and nights of sinking into vocalized and un-vocalized books from the Hadassim library.

One of the students of the graduating class of the Hadassim High School, which operated side by side with the Ulpan, was Shevach Weiss, who was about my age. In later years, Shevach would go on to become the Speaker of the Knesset and Israel's ambassador to Poland. He was very friendly towards with me, and I told him about my love of literature and about my dream to translate Arabic poetry into Hebrew, and perhaps also to become a poet in my own right. One evening there was a big graduation party for the school, and Shevach stood on the dais to read the poem *The Raven* by Edgar Alan Poe, translated by Ze'ev Jabotinsky. The reading of that translation moved me to the core. Since I knew the poem in its English original, I could overcome the challenge of decoding unfamiliar phrases in Jabotinsky's translation. The dizzying rhythmic beat of the poem, masterfully preserved in the translation, resonated in my head for many days, and the following day I approached Shevach and asked him for the text he had read. In those days there were no copy machines, and Shevach did not seem to want to let go of the poem. I remember that the name "Ze'ev Jabotinski" shed some of its negative connotations in my mind, being that he was one of the great Jewish right-wing Zionists of all times. At least culturally speaking, that man now struck me as the incarnation of European broadmindedness, cosmopolitanism, not to mention a great master of the Hebrew language. I went to the local library and searched for Jabotinsky's writings. I found an old copy of the novel *Samson*, which he had written in the 1920s. With the help of an old Hebrew dictionary, I started reading the book. Slowly but persistently, I finished reading it in about two weeks. I believe I managed to follow the basic plot of the novel, although I did not succeed in discerning the allegorical/ideological subtext that I am sure was present between the lines. I was very proud upon completion of the novel, since this was the first Hebrew book I had read on my own initiative, not to mention the fact that it was an un-vocalized text aimed at experienced readers of Hebrew.

Let me recount another personal experience from my time at Hadassim. One of the girls at the regular school, a fifteen- or sixteen-year-old Holocaust survivor named Sarah, lived in a wooden shack next door to the Ulpan. She had a crush on me, and every time she saw me she would try to approach me and start a conversation about this and that. Since her room was on the second floor of her shack, she would call down to my room on the ground floor, and the image reminded me of the balcony scene in Shakespeare's *Romeo and Juliet*. Finally I figured out that she was flirting with me, but since I had no experience with the opposite sex, as I recounted in *Baghdad, Yesterday*, I was of the opinion that the advances had to come from the man, and that the girl – even a full-fledged woman – was not allowed to initiate romantic forays. She should wait for the young man's advances, and then, even if she was interested in a relationship, it was best for her not to respond immediately. Something therefore seemed not quite right in Sarah's growing advances. One day she invited me on a walk through the grounds, and I agreed, though I hoped that she would take me through the dark field route and not through the well-lit main paths, lest we be seen together. But she insisted, that we take the main path. I was confused, and the next day I approached Shevach Weiss, who was my only friend there besides my classmates at the Ulpan, and I asked him, almost in a complaining voice, what to do with a girl who starts "coming on" to you. From his answer I realized that he understood very well the reason for my distress. "In a civilized society, the girl is also allowed to initiate a relationship with the boy. It is not only the right of men!" Shevach answered.

Upon completion of the Ulpan in December 1951, nine months after my arrival in Israel, I received a special gift from the teaching staff –

a box of "Elite" brand chocolates – and heard praises about my dedication as a student (something I had never heard in Iraq, since I had not been a dedicated student there!). The comforting feeling washed over me that I had already mastered the Hebrew language quite well, and so I began to focus my next steps on the almost methodical continuation of my language studies. I decided to systematically read the great works of modern Hebrew literature, and at the same time to persevere in the study of my favorite chapters of the Hebrew Bible, such as the *Song of Songs* and the book of *Amos*, which I could now for the first time read in the original language (in the past I was familiar with the Bible mainly through the Arabic translations of American missionaries in Beirut, and sometimes through the standard English translation).

The firm knowledge of Arabic language and grammar I had brought with me from Iraq is what helped me master Hebrew quickly. Even in the Ulpan, I would sometimes argue with the teachers about matters of Hebrew grammar, and occasionally the teacher even conceded that I was right. When I joined the Israeli army in March 1952, I served in a ground unit of the air force alongside Israeli-born soldiers, both women and men. For some reason, many of the female soldiers had completed a year of teachers' training. Once I overheard two of them arguing about a question related to the Hebrew language. I interjected and they were surprised to discover that, despite my still-foreign accent, I demonstrated a firm knowledge of the subject at hand. The rumor quickly spread that I was a linguistic expert, and I became an arbiter in matters of Hebrew language. Two and a half years at a military base, where most of the soldiers were Israeli-born, also helped me overcome the problem of the accent. "Helped", I say, although I am not sure this is the correct word in this context, since one of the changes that occurred in my accent was the loss of the gutturals (primarily the consonants Het and 'Ayin), which I affected in order to sound more like the native Israelis. This made it somewhat difficult for me to return to the Middle Eastern pronunciation upon my acceptance as a member of the Academy of Hebrew Language in Jerusalem at the beginning of the 1960s. There I felt that even if all (or almost all) of the members of the Academy spoke with an Ashkenazi accent, I, as an Arab Jew, needed to speak in Hebrew in its Middle Eastern version, and that the use of the

Ashkenazi accent would sound like an imitation. And so I returned to speak gutturally.

CHAPTER

4

"THE EARTH SHALL RISE ON NEW FOUNDATIONS"

I decided to join the Israeli Communist Party (Maki) in September 1954, even before completing my mandatory military service. I was an active party member for about four years, and I kept up my connections with friends in the party and with the literary supplement of *Kol Ha'am* (the Party's Hebrew-language newspaper) even after I stopped being a member. Only in 1968, when the Russian army invaded Prague in an attempt to trample the winds of democracy that were blowing in Czechoslovakia, did I decide upon a complete divorce from communism. I do not regret or apologize for my four years in Maki, and I am still on good terms with many of the friends I made there. Nonetheless, from time to time, I wonder about what was so magnetizing for me in the idea of communism. After all, in 1954 there were enough elements in Soviet communism to repel a person with a democratic worldview (or, more correctly, social-democratic, in the original meaning of the phrase). Moreover, the Soviet Union had already begun to speak about Israel as a sworn enemy, after a brief "honeymoon" that lasted for a year or two in 1948 and 1949.

Stalin (who died in 1953) was exposed as an avowed anti-Semite following the Night of the Murdered Writers and the Doctors' Plot in which (mostly Jewish) Soviet doctors were accused of a conspiracy to poison the leaders of the Soviet Union (incidentally, the doctors' trial was called off a short time after Stalin's death). Unmistakable anti-Semitic tones were also exposed during the 1952 Prague show trials, during which Mordechai Oren, a member of a Shomer Ha-Tzair

22

kibbutz and one of the leading left-wing activists in Israel, was sentenced to a long prison term. Why, in those of all days, did I decide to jump into the murky waters of communism? Was I not aware of the lacunae within the Soviet (and Israeli) brands of communism? I was aware, in fact, and perhaps it was because of this awareness that I insisted upon joining the "wrong" side, in order to make the statement that I had not given up on the great dream, the utopian dream. The abandonment of the dream in its Bolshevik version (the operative word being "dream" and not the realization of it) would be an admission that the idea of socialism and equality was dead and buried for good.

I was ten years old when Hitler's army succumbed to Stalin-led Soviet resistance. I remember the evenings in Baghdad when my father and I would sit next to our big Philips radio receiver with its flashing bulbs and listen to the news of the War. My father used a small school atlas to follow the names mentioned on the BBC. When the back of the Wehrmacht was broken, we understood that the imminent danger to us, the Jews of the Middle East, was gone for good, and that Rommel's intended invasion of Egypt and beyond would not come to be, since the Germans were now obliged to transfer the bulk of their forces to the Russian front. Our joy at this was etched in my consciousness in the form of thanks and appreciation for the Soviet Union and its leadership. These were our true protectors. They fought like lions to defeat the Nazi beast.

In 1948 (still in Iraq), with the outbreak of the war in Israel, an anti-Jewish wave swept through Baghdad, led by the radical nationalist parties (which in the past had collaborated with the pro-Nazi regime of Rashid Ali in 1941). The Iraqi Communist Party, which unconditionally accepted Stalin's orders to support the Palestine Partition Plan, fought tooth and nail to protect the Jews of Baghdad. Its members carried signs reading "The Jews are our brothers, the Zionists are our enemy", and their activists (prominent among whom were many young Jews) did all they could to thwart the possibility of another pogrom, like the Farhud of 1941.

In that same year, many of the young Jews marched in the demonstrations against the renewal of the Portsmouth Treaty between Britain and Iraq. The participation of these Jews (and even, in one case, the head of the Jewish community, Rabbi Sasson Khedoury) was seen by the Iraqi Left as proof of the cross-ethnic unity of the Iraqi people in the national struggle, and of the absurdity of the claims of the nationalistic Iraqi Right.

After arriving in Israel, I was faced with the fact that the Palestinians who had remained in the State of Israel were stuck between a rock and a hard place, between the Arabs who saw them as "traitors" for staying in the despised Jewish state, and the Israelis who saw them as potential enemies. Maki was the only party whose ranks included both Jews and Arabs. This fact brought me even closer to Maki and its activists (and in particular to the writers and poets of the party), and as will be told in the next chapter, I began, along with my friend David Semah, to work toward the establishment of a literary circle of Arabic-writing Jews in Tel Aviv, under the unofficial auspices of Emile Habiby and Sami Michael, two of Maki's most prominent activists in those days. Although I was drawn in by the achievements of the kibbutz movement in Israel, and in particular by the kibbutzim of the Shomer Ha-Tzair movement, I could not bring myself to join its political party, Mapam, since only Jews could be full members in it. Throughout 1953, there was a critical struggle between the right and left wings of Mapam, in which Dr. Moshe Sneh stood at the head of the left faction. The left faction, and in particular members who were kicked out of the Shomer Ha-Tzair kibbutzim due to their support of Sneh's line, founded a small party of their own in 1953 called "Smol" (simply, "Left"), and produced an excellent political weekly by the same name. A friend of mine, an Egyptian Jew who was a soldier in my unit, and myself considered joining Smol, but then it became clear that they were about to join Maki (and that indeed happened). Thus, at the end of a sleepless night of mulling the subject over, we both decided to join forces with Maki.

At the time I was living in Bat Yam, a suburb of Tel Aviv, in my family's apartment in a small public housing complex. Soon, almost by chance, quite a few of the kibbutz exiles arrived there. They were Israeli-born for the most part (although many of the veteran members of Maki were Eastern European immigrants who had arrived after World War II). I became friendly with a few of them, and I would go out on Friday afternoons with another member of the Maki branch, to go door to door trying to sell copies of the Friday edition of *Kol Ha'am* and speak with the residents of these apartments to try and dissuade them from the anti-communist incitement that was so rampant in Israel at the time. Most of the residents stuck to their firm anti-communist stance, but to their credit it should be said that in most cases they were not uncivil with the communists who appeared at their doorsteps, even in the following years, with the Soviet Union's explicit support of the Arab side and the signing of the Czech–Egyptian arms deal.

Even though It was difficult (almost impossible) to convince the residents of Bat Yam and other Jewish towns to change their opinions, the very fact of the never-ending argument conducted during "distribution" hours reinforced and deepened my belief in the justice of my path, and in my powers of persuasion.

As I will relate below, by the mid-50s I was devoting a lot of time to writing for the literary column of *Kol Ha'am* and also, on occasion, for the Arabic-language *Al-Jadid*. Thus I was liberated from organizational duties in the party, and only the Friday distributions and the weekly party cell meetings remained an unremitting duty.

There were, of course, times when all members of the party were mobilized for a particular cause, usually at times of crisis. To recall one such moment: In 1956 the Hungarian popular uprising against Soviet hegemony broke out and placed us all in a difficult position. Hungarian communist leader Imre Nagy declared his country's neutrality in the intra-bloc conflict, and the Soviet armies put down the uprising and executed him. It took the Party in Israel many weeks to recover from the Hungarian tragedy, and to construct a web of justifications for the Soviet invasion of one of the "popular democracies"; for instance, by placing all the blame on "fascist" elements in Hungary, which were themselves remnants of Hungarian fascism of the 1930s and 40s.

I would also like to mention, if only briefly, two events connected to the Soviet Union itself. In 1954, the 19th congress of the Soviet Communist Party took place. In his speech, Georgy Malenkov, Stalin's successor as leader of the Soviet Union and its single party, stated that "Soviet agriculture is a catastrophe". It is hard to describe the shock that seized me upon hearing this sentence. After all, shouldn't any communist anywhere in the world sing the praises of Soviet agriculture and how it had saved the peoples of the Soviet Union from hunger and allowed them to live in prosperity? Some of us could even tell you how many tractors and how many combines each of the Soviet republics had. And here the most authoritative source was telling us that the situation on the agricultural front was catastrophic. At first thought, such a subject should not make or break one's faith in an entire system, but the very feeling that for years I had been fed false information, and that I myself spread this lie, triggered a bitter disappointment and disillusionment in my "spiritual homeland", the Soviet Union.

And in February 1956, at the 20th Congress of the Soviet Party, the speech of the new leader, Nikita Khrushchev, rocked the foundations when we discovered to our horror that everything we thought we knew about the "legendary" Stalin and about his rule was based on lies. It was a simultaneously corrupt and tyrannical regime. Stalin was one of the greatest tyrants in human history. Neither was Lenin, the glorified leader of the Bolshevik Revolution, exactly an exemplary character. Now, those who had been around long enough began to recall the 1930s and the series of trials that Stalin held and the purges of the highest ranks of the Soviet leadership, culminating in the murder of Trotsky by Stalin's agents in Mexico. It took time and great energy for the leaders of the communist parties to get some of their party members back to the routine of party work, with claims such as "But let us not forget that, were it not for Stalin and his perseverance, we would never have been able to rid the world of Hitler and international fascism!"

In that same year, 1956, "our own" Suez–Sinai war broke out. During the war I was called up to my military unit, which remained on the home front, and when I returned home at the end of the war I once again found a party lacking in unity and discipline: on the Arab side – a growing identification with Nasserism and total identification with the Soviet pro-Arab position. Among the Jewish members there was an uproar of condemnation of Israel for joining the declining colonial powers, Britain and France, but several of these members took exception with the Soviet Union's firm stance against Israel, which was more than a little anti-Semitic. In the two years immediately following the war a great effort was made by the leaders of Maki (Mikunis, Sneh, Habiby, Vilenska, Vilner) to restore unity in the Party; and only the rift that formed between Nasser and the Soviet Union at the end of the 1950s, following the overthrow of Qassem in Iraq, brought about a rapprochement between the Arabs and Jews of Maki (the Soviet Union now openly supported the Republican regime in Iraq and thus annoyed Nasser and his millions of supporters in the Arab world). As for me personally, the Iraqi coup of 1958 was the event that turned my interest from what was happening in Israel to the events in Iraq. In Baghdad the communists ruled the streets, and they had almost exclusive influence in the media as well. They supported General Qassem, the hesitant democrat, and sided with the revolution he headed. Qassem himself, however, was wary of the growing strength of the communists, whom he feared might take power into their own hands. And since he had not built the popular support base necessary for being a true democratic leader, he was left frighteningly alone, ultimately paving the way for the nationalistic right to stage a coup against him and trample his regime in one fell swoop in 1963. Qassem himself was summarily executed in front of the television cameras. I followed the events in Baghdad closely, since I had been there myself only a decade earlier.

In October 1958 I enrolled at Tel Aviv University. The university was established without Ben-Gurion's blessing (he apparently feared that a university in Tel Aviv would diminish the primacy of the Hebrew University and of Jerusalem). The new university was housed in a temporary building in the area of Abu Kabir (Jaffa), with only a few departments at first. Since it did not yet have a department of Arabic or Middle Eastern studies, I signed up for the Hebrew literature and Jewish history departments. Later I transferred from the literature department to the Hebrew language department, where I found my place and graduated with distinction. Although the new university did not have a substantial university library, I immersed myself in my studies and holed myself up in the small library until closing time. At the time I was working as a clerk at a bank near the Tel Aviv central bus station, and I traveled by bicycle back and forth between the bank and the university. These two places, the bank and the university, took up all of my days and evenings, and my weekends were spent on homework. Most of the subjects I was now studying were new to me, since I had never studied in a Jewish-Israeli school, and my knowledge of Jewish history was very superficial. At Tel Aviv University, I studied different episodes in Jewish history, but I was most fascinated by the Second Temple Period (of which the foremost professor was Joshua Efron, a remarkable scholar, strict in his teaching style but kindly in his relations with students); and the period of the Ottoman rule (the leading professor in this field was Zvi Ankori, who was an expert on Karaite communities in the Ottoman Empire and beyond).

While in the Hebrew language department, I was impressed by the erudition of great scholars such as Yehoshua Blau, Yehezkel Kutscher, Shelomo Morag, and others. Paradoxically, I learned the grammar and syntax of biblical Hebrew entirely without having a firm knowledge of the Hebrew biblical text. What I had read in the Bible previously was in either Arabic or English translation. I labored over the biblical grammar book of Gesenius-Kautsch (in its English translation), whose fine print and many pages paid due attention to almost every tiny variation and unique form in the biblical text. Later, when I read the original Hebrew text of the Bible for the first time in an orderly fashion, I discovered to my surprise and delight that almost all of the text was familiar to me in its grammatical context thanks to the learned notes of Gesenius-Kautsch.

My obsession with my studies (like a thirsty person who finally reaches a spring) alongside my work at the bank, which I could not stop at that time, did not allow me to continue my activities in Maki, and I therefore notified the party cell that I would not be able to commit to the minimum demanded of a member, including the distribution hours and the weekly meetings. From now my only party-affiliated activity would be to write in its literary publications.

Perhaps my double occupation provided a convenient excuse for distancing myself from direct political activity – although I did not stop seeing myself as someone who was concerned about current events. I swore not to stop supporting humane socialism, or, if you will, humane communism. The existing alternative, of accepting the terms of the capitalist world in its various regimes, was never acceptable to me. Therefore for several years I remained a passive and tentative supporter of the "world of tomorrow", to be precise – up until 1968. That year I was a student at Oxford. From the small television set at home I eagerly followed the democratic revolt in Czechoslovakia under the leadership of Alexander Dubček. That revolution ended, like the others, with Soviet tanks rolling into the streets of Prague and stamping out the democratic movement there. From that day I stopped seeing myself as a supporter, or even a friend, of the world communist movement. The Soviet tanks destroyed the dream of "democratic communism" for me, once and for all.

CHAPTER

5

LOVERS OF ARABIC IN THE FIRST HEBREW CITY

"The Tel Aviv Arabic Literary Circle", which met intermittently for two or three years in the mid-fifties, was not, in and of itself, a group or an event that left a profound impression on its participants or on the general public. Nonetheless, I dedicate a chapter of this book to it, if only as a curiosity (an Arabic club in the so-called first Hebrew city!); but more importantly because, in the short period of the club's existence, I underwent a number of changes (as did several of my friends) in my relation to questions of language and literature. This was not necessarily a direct result of the existence of the "circle". As we shall presently see, it may even have occurred in spite of it.

First let me dedicate a few words to my partner in the establishment of the circle, the late David Semah. David, a close friend, was a year my elder. He was a distant relative, but it was not in a family context that our friendship blossomed. Our acquaintance began in 1949, a year before he immigrated to Israel, in early 1950, as I recall. He left Baghdad for good about a year before I did, i.e., before the passage of the Law of Renunciation of Nationality (*tasqit*), which would allow most of the Iraqi Jewish community to reach Israel in an orderly fashion. It was in 1948 that David transferred from the Alliance Israélite Universelle School, where he had been until then, to the Shammash High School, where I was a student. I was extremely happy to discover him at my school, because I had found out (through common friends) that he was a dedicated poet and an unparalleled expert in the difficult and complex theory of Arabic meter. We became fast friends upon his arrival at Shammash, and we spent our short daily recesses together. I encouraged David to submit his poems

29

to the Baghdad press, where my poems were published (under a pseudonym) on occasion. We must have been the only ones in all of Shammash School trying to write and publish Arabic poetry. Most of the students had little to do with literature. They were preparing themselves for "a practical life" and studied the required material in Arabic literature only because it was part of the matriculation exams (*i'dadiya*). We were even subject to the occasional ridicule of our peers in and out of school as a result of our enthusiastic devotion to Arabic literature and language.

On one occasion, whilst still in Baghdad, David showed me page proofs of a book that had almost been published, but that had been decided against at the last minute. The first half of the book featured David's poems, while the second half was prose by his collaborator (whose name I cannot recall). The project was not cancelled for literary reasons; and as far as I know it was his partner who had gotten cold feet, fearing that the publication would cause him trouble – not political trouble per se (the book was the furthest thing from politics), but that the very appearance of a book whose writers' names were Jewish (those were the days of the 1948 war in Palestine) seemed problematic.

One fine day at the end of a year of very close friendship, David disappeared from my life, and I soon understood that he had crossed the border on his way to Israel via Iran. I felt abandoned, since we had made many plans together. David didn't tell me about his plans to come illegally to Israel, since he had been sworn to absolute secrecy.

A year later, in March 1951, came my turn to leave Iraq and come to Israel, in the framework of Operation Ezra and Nehemia.[2] Upon my arrival, along with hundreds of other immigrants, to the Sha'ar Ha-Aliyah transit camp near Haifa, I immediately tried to find David, but with no luck. Two days later David himself found his way to the communal tent where I was staying. The meeting was an emotional one, and in the joy of the reunion, David agreed to spend the night at my place. We fell asleep side by side on a simple immigrants' mattress. Most of his family members had already arrived in Israel and settled in the Hatikva neighborhood next to Tel Aviv, in a modest, one-room apartment. David himself worked in a fountain-

---

2 This was the name given to the airlift operation of the Jews of Iraq in 1950–1951 (named after the biblical characters from the time of King Koresh).

pen factory (this was before the advent of ballpoint pens) on Ha-Aliyah Street, close to where he lived. His literary aspirations had been pushed aside; after all, who in the Holy Land needed an Arabic writer or poet in the Jewish state? And where would he publish his poems now? And who would read them? He had not yet sufficiently mastered the Hebrew language in order to try and write in it; even when he did learn Hebrew properly over the course of time, David avoided using the language for his literary endeavors and limited his Hebrew writing to academic articles, as he became a professor at Haifa University in subsequent years.

During his first years in Israel, his criticism grew – of the situation there (all the more now that he himself had fallen into the proletarian class) and in particular of the State's attitude to the Arab minority and its culture. We returned to this subject over and over again in our long conversations, which stretched late into the night on weekends (both of us served in the Israel Defense Forces [IDF] in different places between 1952 and 1954, and it was primarily on weekends that we met).

What, indeed, were the Arabic publications available in Israel at that time? In the Tel Aviv area there was the daily *al-Yawm*, which reflected the views of the government and targeted the Arab minority. Its literary section, in our opinion, left much to be desired. In Haifa, by contrast, there was the weekly *al-Ittihad*, the Arabic-language journal of the Israeli Communist Party, whose editors included talented writers such as Emile Habiby and Jabra Nicola. Sami Michael, who had arrived from Iraq a few years earlier, was also on the editorial board of *al-Ittihad* in those days. They published works of greater literary value than those that appeared in *al-Yawm*, though their subject matter struck us at first as too political and as emphasizing only the negative aspects of the new country – such as the suffering of the Arab masses who had remained in Israel after the establishment of the State, or the misery of the residents of the immigrant transit camps, the masses of whom were arriving in those days from Arab countries. Although we believed such depressing descriptions could encourage the reader to join in a positive struggle to change the situation, they could also have the opposite effect. Still, we preferred to read *al-Ittihad* and its literary supplement, which first appeared in 1952. At the end of 1953, this supplement became an independent literary monthly called *al-Jadid*, edited by Jabra Nicola and featuring Emile Habiby as one of its regular contributors. The latter was our kind of writer – a witty master of the treasures of the classical language, but one who did not shy away from employing the basics of spoken Arabic (which writers generally avoided using in their "respectable" literary writing). We thus became familiar with the principles of *al-Ittihad* and of Maki in general, even if we had not yet joined ranks with the Maki activists, many of whom had come from Iraq and lived and operated in the transit camps near Tel Aviv and Petah Tikva.

One of the first issues of *al-Jadid* featured a report on a conference in which matters of literature had been discussed. Participating in the conference, which was held under Maki's auspices, were some of the prominent Arab writers who sympathized with the party. (Most Arab intellectuals tended toward Maki.) Emile Habiby summarized the discussion in his brilliant and pungent style: the lecture was general in nature and it discussed, from a Marxist perspective, the fate of Arabic literature in the country, and its attitude toward the new reality that had been created with the establishment of the State of Israel, in which part of the Palestinian people lived. David and I read Habiby's words with great interest, and very much identified with what he wrote. We decided to send a letter to the editor of *al-Jadid*, and also, for the first time, considered establishing a literary circle for Arabic writers in the Tel Aviv area. On one of those weekends, the two of us sat on the balcony of David's apartment and painstakingly wrote the letter or manifesto, the main points of which I translate here as it appeared in the March 1954 issue of *al-Jadid*:

We are from Iraq and were previously engaged in Arabic literature. Several of us published poems and stories in Iraq and in Israel, and these have been broadcast on the radio [we were referring to a poem of David's that he had read aloud on an Arabic broadcast in Israel on the occasion of one of the holidays]. But we quickly tired of the decadent bourgeois culture. Therefore, we entirely abandoned this kind of literature and turned toward a militant literature that was free of decadent influences. However our association with Arabic literary circles since came to a halt. Some of us stopped writing while others nearly gave up on the possibility of someday writing Arabic literature again. Then along came *al-Jadid* and infused us with a real sense of hope.

Our wish is to convene a group of friends to be the core of a literary circle associated with *al-Jadid*, with the goal of bringing us closer to activist Arabic literature and exposing a group of young people to a socially committed literature; perhaps they will even be able to contribute something of their own to this effort. Our intention is to strengthen the solidarity and camaraderie between the two peoples – Jewish and Arab; and the two literatures – Hebrew and Arabic. This will be done through mutual translation of the two languages and familiarization of the Jewish readership with Arabic literature, and the Arab public with Hebrew literature.

The Tel Aviv Arabic literary circle quickly took shape. Some two months after the letter was published (alongside an enthusiastic response from the journal's editors), we convened the first meeting of the circle on the balcony of the Semah family apartment on a pleasant spring evening. We tried to make the event as formal as possible, insofar as we could achieve "formality". As the founders, David and I (both of us, as has been said, were soldiers in the regular service) ran the meeting. Participating were a dozen or so friends from the literati. Besides them, two representatives of *al-Jadid* came from Haifa – Jabra Nicola, the editor, and the Iraqi-Jewish writer Sami Michael, who was one of the best short-story writers on the local Arabic literary scene at the time.

We did not take notes at the meeting, but I recall the "greetings" of Jabra and Sami, who did not make do with general warm remarks, but also engaged in a literary and ideological give-and-take, each in his own style, each according to his own worldview. During the course of the discussion, they and the other participants raised questions regarding our growing distance from the Arabic literary sources, and the need for literary action and writing that would reflect the dramatic change that had taken place in the lives of the new immigrants. Nicola, as a veteran, experienced Marxist, also spoke about the "principles" of proletarian literature, and about the importance of language, the mother tongue, in the literary act.

I have no notes either from the second meeting, which took place a few weeks later, but in the meantime our friend Shimon Ballas joined the circle and immediately volunteered to take on some of the organizational and administrative responsibilities. In the meantime, Sami Michael published a programmatic article in *al-Jadid* (July 1954 issue) summing up his speech from the first meeting; it turns out that even then he gave great consideration to the linguistic questions facing a writer skilled in writing in one language, upon moving into a new linguistic environment. In the end of his article, Michael writes:

> Realism in literature obliges the immigrant writers to deal with the problems facing the masses that surround them, and to march at all times in the mainstream and not at the margins. They must contribute to the creation of a progressive Hebrew culture that is faithful to the interests of the Israeli people while respecting other peoples. These writers are faced with the choice between being simultaneously Jewish and internationalist, and slipping down the slopes of cosmopolitanism.

Michael's ideological jargon in the above passage is not surprising, as it perfectly reflects the modalities of communist discourse in those days (e.g., the distinction between *positive* "internationalism" and *negative* "cosmopolitanism"). What is surprising in this paragraph is that Michael sees one of the roles of the writers who came from Iraq as creating a progressive and humanist "*Hebrew* culture", despite the fact that none of the members of the circle was comfortable with Hebrew literature or yet wrote in Hebrew.

The third meeting of the circle, held in September 1954, is properly documented thanks to an extensive report on its deliberations, published in the December issue of *al-Jadid*. Sami Michael once again came from Haifa to the meeting, since the discussion was to revolve around the point he had raised earlier in the above article in *al-Jadid* – namely, the problem of reflecting reality and the question in which language a recently-arrived immigrant writer in the Hebrew state should write. Shimon Ballas opened the discussion, and no less than eight members of the circle participated. Most of them supported Michael's approach and believed that one must master the Hebrew language and eventually also write in it. And what of the Arabic language, in whose name the circle had been formed? This was, indeed, the natural literary language of the members of the circle, but beyond that was the writer's need to communicate with the people in whose midst he lived, and his responsibility to reflect reality and broaden the horizons of his readers. For that purpose, whoever was to continue writing literature could not conscionably hide behind the saying that was common then in left-wing circles: "Language is not the main thing; the content is more important". Rather, he must demonstrate "dynamism", which in this case meant a transition into Hebrew sooner rather than later. These things were not said explicitly, but in David Semah's remarks as they appear in the report, he cites Sami Michael as having stated that the immigrants from Arab lands had to learn Hebrew and write in it (this was not explicit in Michael's July article, but it is there between the lines). Semah adds that, unlike a mathematical problem that has a singular solution, the writer is free to take whatever course he chooses.

The closing words quoted in my name in the report are as follows:

We must follow with interest the continued development of Hebrew literature while supporting Arabic literature in Israel. The importance of the mutual translation of the two languages [Arabic and Hebrew] is inseparable from the fact that such translations have the ability to counter the calls for further wars and strengthen understanding between the two peoples.

The subject of mutual translation, which I mention in the above quote, possessed me like a spirit for many years; it was one of the things that pushed me to devote myself to literary translation and in particular to the translation of modern Arabic poetry into Hebrew. But to continue with the story of the circle in the months immediately following these discussions: the circle met on and off for two more years, dealing with general problems and in addition dedicating a few meetings to a discussion of Arabic works written by its members. In 1955, some four years after the massive immigration from Iraq, the club petered out. The members' fervent embrace of their Arab roots gradually dwindled by force of reality. There was an urgent need to learn Hebrew, not only in the literary context but also, and more powerfully, in daily life — for the sake of finding proper employment and a future in the new country. As a final note I will say that in one of the final meetings of the club, it was decided to change the name to "The Tel Aviv Hebrew-Arabic Literature Circle", with the purpose of attracting audiences whose mother tongue was not Arabic. This was in spite of the opposition of some of the members, among whom, as I recall, was Shimon Ballas, who took the stance that we must continue in the original direction of the circle and stick to Arabic language and literature.

At the end of the 1950s and in the decades following, a few members of the club did indeed turn to Hebrew and wrote most of their literary works in that language. It is interesting that the first one to publish an important work in Hebrew was none other than Shimon Ballas, whose novel *The Transit Camp* appeared in 1964 in the prestigious People's Library series. Approximately ten years later, Sami Michael's first Hebrew novel, *Equal and More Equal*, appeared. David Semah and I turned to academia and the study of Arabic literature. In 1959, David published a collection of Arabic poems called "Until the Spring Comes" but afterward wrote fewer and fewer poems in this language. I turned to writing poetry in Hebrew but, too, stopped this at the end of the decade. As for the rest of the members of the club – I lost touch with most of them over the years. Many of them abandoned literary activity and immersed themselves in "practical matters", some even becoming very successful in their professions.

And in order to complete the picture, let me recall the names of two Iraqi-born writers who were not members of the circle, in fact, who were not yet known as writers in the years the club existed. I refer to Samir Naqqash (1937–2004) and Yitzhak Bar-Moshe (1927–2003). These two talented storytellers did not appear in public during their first twenty years in Israel, but after the Six Day War their Arabic-language stories began to flow like a river. They each published, over the course of time, some twenty lengthy, dense Arabic books; and this was after the Iraqi immigrants themselves had for the most part stopped reading in Arabic. In the last years of his life and following his death in 2004, Samir Naqqash aroused great interest in Iraq and in the Arabic press around the world. He never saw himself as an Israeli writer; he insisted on writing on the covers of those of his books *whose themes were Iraqi* "an Iraqi story".

As one who admires this writer's talent, I hope to see the day that his oeuvre will be inscribed in the history of contemporary Arabic literature and be translated into Hebrew.

CHAPTER

6

DAYS WITH
ALEXANDER PENN

I met the poet Alexander Penn for the first time at his apartment at the end of Dizengoff Street in Tel Aviv sometime around 1954. Prior to this visit, I had mailed him a few poems that I had translated from Arabic into Hebrew for the literary supplement of *Kol Ha'am*, and I received notification by mail (the presence of a telephone in every home was not then common) asking me to pay a call on Penn one morning, in order to discuss the possibility of publishing the material. I knew that he was the literary editor of Maki's daily newspaper.

Alexander Penn, in the flesh! Despite my being a new immigrant, I had already heard a lot about the man, his poetry, and his life. At music lessons in my Ulpan at Hadassim, we had learned "Adama, Admati" ("Land, My Land"), an iconic Zionist song. On another occasion I saw his picture in *Al-Ittihad*, the weekly journal of Maki. And then I began asking myself how his Zionism and his communism coexisted. And then I heard stories, some of them true, some made-up, about his alleged bohemian lifestyle, about his being the great playboy of Tel Aviv, and about his adventures throughout the thirties. I was told (incorrectly) that one could see him if one peeked into Café Kassit. I peeked in and didn't see him, although I did happen upon a group of famous writers among whom I recognized Avraham Shlonsky, Nathan Alterman, and several other, lesser known, writers.

The meeting to which I was called in Penn's apartment was therefore an honor beyond my wildest dreams. I took two or three poems I had written in Hebrew (these must have been the first poems I had written in the language); Penn skipped the introductions and went straight to the matter of translated poems, asking me if I would allow him to edit the Hebrew (mainly corrections in meter and rhyme). I agreed, and even showed him the poems I had written myself. He perused them and chose one poem, which he offered to publish in his supplement after giving it a "retouche". I hesitated for a moment. How could I let another person, as experienced as he may have been, make corrections in the language of a poem that was originally written in Hebrew and that was supposed to reflect "voices" straight from nature (I believe that the poem Penn chose was "Where is the Spring?")? Even so, I agreed, and when the poem came out in the newspaper two weeks later, I saw that my reservations had not been unfounded. Penn's style, in particular the frequent use of assonant rhymes, overshadowed my language. In the poems I had translated, on the other hand, the corrections were less fundamental.

I made my next visit to Penn's apartment uninvited. One day, mid-week at twilight, I rang at his apartment door and his wife Rachel opened it. I saw him standing facing the mirror and dressing, as if he were about to go out. "I came to show you some more poems that I translated", I said. "That is nice, young man", he said, "but now I am going out. Perhaps you can accompany me to the 'Medura' Club? We can speak more leisurely there". I accompanied him, in my army uniform, and from that evening on, for a year or more, I would meet him at the club (which belonged to the Kibbutz Ha-Meuhad movement, just as the "Tzavta" Club belonged to the Shomer Ha-Tzair) on every free evening I had from my unit in Tel Aviv. As we walked along Dizengoff Street, all eyes, of men and women alike, were drawn to the always handsome man who marched erectly next to me (even if his gait sometimes betrayed a slight limp, the result of the diabetes from which he suffered for many years).

The frequency of our meetings varied. They were less frequent in periods when I would meet and start spending time with a girlfriend; but in times when I was free of this kind of relationship I would stop by to see Alexander Penn, wherever he was. In his company I met all sorts of men and women. Few, if any, were from the world of literature or culture, but rather friends from days past (some spoke only Russian), who had no apparent interest in literature or language. Penn, it seemed to me, was distancing himself from the company of writers, both his peers and those younger than him, as if he were tired of them for ideological reasons. When we were alone, our conversations naturally revolved around literature and politics. Today I realize that Penn never truly opened up to me; he did not share his thoughts and doubts (which he must have had, despite his reassuring façade, which always seemed to boast a long and varied life experience, although he was only in his fifties). Later on he stopped serving as the literary editor of *Kol Ha'am* (the responsibility went over to Michael Harsegor, later Professor Harsegor, an expert in European History). I would show him poems I had written and listen to his feedback, which he now gave as constructive criticism rather than meddling with the structure of the poetic text.

In 1957, Penn's collection of poems *Along the Way* was festively published by "Science and Life", a Party-affiliated publisher that might well have been established for the express purpose of publishing that book. The preparation of the texts, the printing, and the illustrations (by painter Gershon Knispel, also a member of the Party) took many months. Penn worked hard on the proofs and lay-out, during which time he made many corrections and additions, to the chagrin of the publishers. Here and there I got wind of the arguments between him and Maki chairman, MK Shmuel Mikunis, regarding what was allowed and forbidden in the representative poems of a "proletarian poet", whose muse was to be devoted to "the world of tomorrow". Poems with Jewish content or that somehow identified with the Zionist enterprise were scorned, but Penn insisted upon having the last word (for more on this, see Hagit Halperin's excellent book *The Color of Life: the Life and Work of Alexander Penn*, Tel Aviv 2007 [in Hebrew]).

In 1958, as I noted earlier, I enrolled in the newly established Tel Aviv University, whose courses were held initially in a temporary structure in Abu Kabir. It had been my dream to study at a university from the day I arrived in Israel, and even earlier; but the realization of the dream was deferred time and time again, in part because the only university in the country was located in Jerusalem (and the Technion in Haifa had no humanities faculty). My studies at Abu Kabir took me away from many of the activities that had filled my life in the past, among them my relationship with Penn. From time to time, when I would happen upon his table at the "Medura", Penn would say something in a scolding tone about how I had abandoned my friends and ask me for a "detailed report" of the mischief I was up to, as he put it.

In 1961 or thereabouts, I began to publish a column in *Kol Ha'am* called "Questions on Language", which dealt with problems in the Hebrew language and tried to guide the reader through the socio-linguistic labyrinth without taking the "say/don't say" approach that was so common among grammarians of the previous generation. Penn would occasionally drop oblique responses to these columns such as: "So we finally have a linguistic column of our own, in which you clarify altogether common matters, but by your enthusiastic tones one would think you had discovered America", he would say. Our last meeting took place in one of the coffee houses around Dizengoff Square. I happened upon him with my American girlfriend, Terrie, later my wife. When I introduced Terrie to Penn he understood that we were considering getting married, and asked me if I had come for his permission in such a matter as well.

From 1965 to 1968 I continued my studies in England, and when I returned to Israel I learned that his health had deteriorated and that he had undergone some major operations. I tried to visit him, but for some reason it did not come to be. In 1970, I received regards from him through a common friend. This friend told me that Penn had read with much interest Issue 47 of Aharon Amir's literary quarterly, *Keshet*, which was devoted to contemporary Arabic literature and which I had edited; and he sent his congratulations.

And now that I have mentioned Aharon Amir and his quarterly *Keshet*, let me mention one praiseworthy literary act of his. In the first issue of *Keshet*, which appeared at the end of 1958, Amir prominently published some of Alexander Penn's poems, thus breaking the unofficial boycott that had been placed by poets and critics of the period on the poet who dared to take jabs both at communism and at some of the deeds and failures of the Zionist state. And while some of the prominent poets avoided contact with Penn, there were also those who maintained their friendship with him despite everything. Among those I recall the late poet Avot Yeshurun, who would meet with Penn (even in public), and about whom Penn spoke positively and whose poetry he advised me to read.

My connection with Penn and with his poetry was most fundamentally for political and ideological reasons, but besides these factors, I appreciate many of the formal elements in his poetry, which have nothing to do with political content. I loved the titillating, refreshing rhythmic beat of his poems ("He was just a simple man / there are countless ones like him"), his unconventional odd assonant rhymes, which made the reader stop and observe the surprising linguistic fabric they wove; the momentum often felt in the complex game of simultaneously similar and different sounds ("the wrath of the sun he did gird / and an easterly vengeful sword; Hagar in the Beer-Sheban desert did err / the water vanished under the orb").

It was good (albeit sad) to see Penn's poetry posthumously reclaim a place of honor in the pantheon of modern Hebrew poetry, not only those poems that were set to music but also his lyrical and lyrical-philosophical poems. The appearance of the complete two-volume edition of his poems in 2006, edited by Hagit Halperin and Uzi Shavit, completes – so I hope – the process of reacceptance (or metaphorical "repatriation"). For many years following the appearance of *Along the Way* (about forty years earlier), not all of Penn's poems could be found in the bookstores, and only partial anthologies, edited by Yossi Gamzu and Uzi Shavit, were available. Penn was an unusual poet, and for that we should recognize his place in the heart of twentieth-century Israeli literature. He died in Tel Aviv in 1972, at the age of sixty-six.

CHAPTER

7

AN INTERRUPTED DIALOGUE

The poet Rashid Hussein was born in 1936 in the Arab village of Musmus next to Umm al-Fahm, in the "Triangle" of Arab villages in the northeast of Israel. After completing his high school studies, he undertook the publication of two collections of his poems. These collections, printed in Nazareth, were called *With the Dawn* (1957) and *Rockets* (1958). He quickly earned a name for himself as an original poet and as an eloquent spokesperson for his people and his homeland. He was employed by the socialist-Zionist Mapam Party as deputy editor of its Arabic-language literary monthly *Al-Fajr* (*The Dawn*), and at the beginning of the 1960s worked for a time at the Arabic edition of Uri Avnery's weekly *Ha'olam Ha'zeh* (*This World*). In 1967 Hussein left Israel for Damascus and later for New York. There he died in 1977 at age forty-three in a fire in his apartment. His remains were brought home and buried in his native village of Musmus.

I developed a friendship with Rashid at the offices of *Al-Fajr*, immediately after he began staying in Tel Aviv. Our friendship was facilitated by my great admiration for his poetic talent, all the more so since I considered him to be the first genuine Arab-Israeli poet. Rashid was the first Palestinian poet to go through the Israeli school system, while those who preceded him (Lubani, Qa'war, Abu-Hanna, 'Abbasi) were already after school age in 1948 when the State of Israel was established. At his Nazareth high school, Rashid was exposed (as were those who came after him, such as Mahmoud Darwish and Samih Al-Qasim) to Hebrew language and literature. Later on the young poet discovered many Israeli intellectuals and writers, many of whom were from the generation known as the "generation of 1948".

My friendship with Rashid was not a simple one. Firstly, he worked for a Zionist party, Mapam, and befriending him would be looked upon as a sort of "deviation" by my many friends in the non-Zionist Maki. Although I wrote several articles for his journal, I always used pseudonyms for fear of criticism on the part of my Palestinian friends in Haifa and Nazareth.

Furthermore, while my political views were more or less identical to those of the Palestinian intellectuals in Maki, between Rashid and myself there was a great disparity. He had come of age in the Nasserite era and was an ardent believer in pan-Arabism and Arab nationalism. Meanwhile, between 1958 and 1963, Iraq was ruled by an anti-Nasserite regime with clear left-wing tendencies. For this reason the Soviet Union showed its preference for Qasem's Iraq over Nasser's Egypt. This situation created a serious rift between the Israeli communists and Arab nationalists of Rashid Hussein's ilk. In his articles in *Al-Fajr*, Rashid launched crushing attacks on the Iraqi regime, on the Soviet Union, and on the Israeli communists. Naturally I was ideologically on the opposite side of Rashid, and our relationship should not logically have withstood that period. But it was precisely in those years – between 1958 and 1960 – that our friendship blossomed, despite the fact that I was then deep in my studies at Tel Aviv University.

Rashid was a pleasant, tall, dark, and affable young man. During the months he spent in Tel Aviv he became friendly with many of the city's writers and journalists. Among these were Binyamin Tammuz and Boaz Evron, both editors for the *Ha'aretz* daily newspaper. These two, along with Ze'ev Schiff (who also worked at *Ha'aretz*), came up with the idea to hold a sort of "summit" meeting between Jewish and Arab writers. Rashid was the contact (and the authority) when it came to the writers from the Galilee and the Triangle. Rashid and Evron asked me if I would be willing to translate the poems – three in all, from Arabic to Hebrew – that would be read at the gathering. I agreed, and I put all my energy into the translations. I delivered the three translated poems to Rashid before the event, which was set to take place on October 9, 1958, in Binyamin Tammuz's studio. Tammuz published an article in the literary supplement of *Ha'aretz* in which he laid out the idea behind the meeting, and later on published Rashid's poem, *The Locked Door*, in my translation. In this short poem the poet complains to his

Jewish friend about how he, an Arab poet, is required to praise the Zionist enterprise and stop complaining. Here is the first stanza of the poem:

> You ask me to describe the beauty of the kibbutz and moshav and
> the Negev because the Yarkon waters were directed to the dry lands?
> But you forgot, my brother, that you locked the door before me
> Do you wish me to be a liar and foolish clown?
> Indeed you locked the door before me
> How then can you demand that I praise
> what has disappeared beyond the door.

This was the first poem read at the gathering. It was followed by two long, pastoral-type poems – *Land* by Hanna Abu-Hanna and *Tale of a Struggle* by 'Issa Lubani. In comparison with Rashid's short poem, the two longer poems struck a dissonant chord among the Jewish writers.

While Rashid Hussein made do with a forceful but polite plea to his Jewish brothers, the two other poets, both of them communists, did not try to hold a dialogue with their Jewish neighbors. Their purpose was to tell the story of the "land" – the key word in Palestinian poetry, to this very day – and they did so in a tone that was both elegiac and militant. Hanna Abu-Hanna, from the village of Reineh near Nazareth, tells in his poem of a young farmer from the Galilee who is in love with a girl from his village, Salma. Over their future and happiness hovers a disaster known as the theft of land; and it is followed by a life of exile and wandering. The poem opens in a pastoral tone: the lush countryside, girls with jugs on their heads. But behind this beauty hides the imminent tragedy of the confiscation of the land by the Israeli authorities. The entire village is in an uproar over the dreadful tidings. At the end of the poem appears the motif of the struggle against the land confiscations – at the time one of Maki's catch phrases in the Arab street.

The final poem, more blunt than the two previous ones, was 'Issa Lubani's *Tale of a Struggle*. The poet came from the destroyed village of Mujaydil, on whose ruins were built the Jewish town of Migdal Ha-Emeq. Lubani and his family fled their village and became refugees in the neighboring city of Nazareth. The poem itself is strewn with autobiographical elements, although fundamentally it is a poem of outcry and struggle that does not spare the perpetrators of the Palestinian tragedy its derogatory words and admonitions: despite the tragedy, the proud and deeply rooted people will not give up, and will get its rights back in this struggle.

Now, a few words about the participants in the meeting. On the Jewish side most of the poets on the Zionist Left (the self-declared representatives of "progressive culture") attended. At their head was Avraham Shlonsky, along with the poets Amir Gilboa, Haim Gouri, Avraham Halfi, and others, as well as the fiction-writers Aharon Megged and Moshe Shamir. Absent from the meeting was the poet Nathan Alterman (who was affiliated with the newspaper *Davar*) as well as a few others who were associated with the Zionist Left. Also missing were the poets of Maki: Alexander Penn, Mordechai Avi-Shaul, and Haya Kadmon, who were not invited to the meeting, and whose marginalization was considered a patriotic act.

On the Arab side, the participants included the three poets whose poems Tammuz read, a few of the prominent writers associated with Maki (in effect, besides those who were affiliated with Maki, there were almost no Arab writers willing to engage in a dialogue), first and foremost being Jabra Nicola, critic and editor of *Al-Jadid*, a fierce intellectual who began his career in writing in the beginning of the 1930s in Jaffa; and also the poet Shakib Jahshan, who was affiliated with the Party. Opposite them was Habib Qahwaji, a poet from the village of Fasuta and one of the leaders of the Palestinian nationalist current in those days, who eventually left the country. Those Arab poets who tended to stay away from politics, such as Michel Haddad from Nazareth, and Habib Zeidan-Shwayri from Kfar Yassif, were not among the participants in the meeting, and they may well not have been invited.

I myself was not invited to participate, in part because I was "only a translator", but also (so I believe) because of my connections with Maki, whose Jewish members were banned. The day after the meeting I rushed to Rashid Hussein and he described to me in great detail what was said and what transpired in Tammuz's studio. Several of the Jewish participants wrote articles and reports in the newspapers: Tammuz in *Ha'aretz*, Megged in the literary bi-weekly, *Massa*, of which he was the editor in those days. Rashid himself published a lengthy response in *Massa* to critic Gabriel Moked's fierce condemnation of what he saw as the politicization of Arabic poetry, which, in Moked's opinion, in most of the cases was not poetry, but a string of slogans (the translated poems themselves were eventually published: Lubani's poem appeared in *Massa* and Abu-Hanna's in *Ha'aretz*).

Later there was an argument between the Maki members, who saw the boycotting of Alexander Penn and his friends as despicable, and the orientalist Michael Assaf, the expert in Arab affairs for *Davar*, whose critique focused on the goal of the meeting's initiators and on the choice of participating poets. And most interesting of all: at the meeting there were discussions of holding further meetings, the first of which would take place in Nazareth and at which the Jewish writers would present their works and opinions. This second meeting never took place, among other things because of the friction that developed between the Arab writers themselves; and between the Maki members and their opponents, in the aforementioned Iraqi context.

One could say that that was the first meeting of note between Jewish-Israeli writers and the representatives of the nascent Palestinian-Israeli literature (this was before the appearance of Darwish and Al-Qasim on the literary stage). From the many details that I collected from Rashid, Evron, and others, I heard frightened reflections from the mouths of the Jewish writers, such as: until now we did not know that such rage, such protest, existed in the Arab public in Israel. And the Arab writers in this society (whom they had not encountered prior to this) were polite people who boasted of their mastery of Hebrew language and culture. It was a fascinating encounter for several of the participants from both sides, although a real dialogue did not develop and did not seem to be on the horizon. Both groups remained firm in their own positions.

What was the mood at the meeting? Since I was not there, I am including excerpts from the fascinating and reliable description by poet Haim Gouri, which was published in *Massa* on October 17, 1958. The following excerpts of the article (which was originally titled "A Meeting Between Four Walls") are reprinted with the permission of the writer:

> Last Thursday I was present at an encounter that took place in Tel Aviv. A few days prior to it I received a letter, signed by two of my friends, in which was written "On Thursday at eight thirty, at the

apartment of X, a meeting will be held with a group of Arab writers and poets. Your presence is requested".

There were many people in the room. I immediately recognized Avraham Shlonsky by his forehead and his graying hair. Among others I recognized Avot Yeshurun and Avraham Halfi, Amir Gilboa, Moshe Shamir, and Aharon Megged, and one woman whose name was Shoshana Sharira, and Binyamin Tammuz, T. Carmi and Ben-Zion Tomer, and one Yitzhak Norman, and Ze'ev Schiff and Boaz Evron ("The Canaanite"). And a lady named Heda, who served coffee with cardamom to the attendees.

I understood that people from different "currents" had been invited. I did not recognize any of the Arabs. They sat on benches and on couches and on the rug, dressed in shirts and suits, and it was difficult at first glance to tell one apart from the next. But I knew that they were all Arabs.

The host stood up and gave a few introductory words: "First let us get acquainted". A young man by the name of Rashid Hussein stood up and read out the names of his colleagues. Unfortunately, I do not remember the names of all of them. There were, among others, Hanna Abu-Hanna and 'Issa Lubani, and Isam Abbasi and Habib Qahwaji, and an older man with graying hair – Jabra Nicola and more . . . about ten of them. Our host introduced the Jewish side.

Then the host read three poems written by the Arabs, translated into Hebrew [by the author of this volume]. Silence resounded between the four walls of the smoke-filled room. A silence that continued for quite some time after our host finished the reading.

The poems ripped in three fell swoops through a closed gate. I cannot judge their poetic merit since they were translated. But their content I understood. They were all three quite similar, three twin brothers. Frightening. One short, two long. Horrifically long: "The destroyed village", "The train of exiles", "The stolen land", "The cruel enemy", "The despised", "The collaborationist traitor", "The hope that the day will come" . . . Here and there were strewn amazing descriptions of nature: morning in the Galilee, sunset. The smoke of the taboun. A young girl carrying a jug on her head.

Shlonsky was somewhat at a loss for words. He spoke about original vs. translation, but at times it seemed like he wanted to say something else . . .

This is the first time, I said to myself, that I am present at such a meeting. Two worlds face to face. I had met Arabs. I had often dined at Arab restaurants, and strolled in their markets, in their villages. I had oftentimes walked through the landscapes in which their existence was marked in sight and sound and smell.

Aharon Megged takes the floor and after him one of theirs. Moshe Shamir speaks slowly and condescendingly. After him one of theirs: "The military government, movement permits, the injustice, the fear. The oppression". "Abdel Nasser does not want war. The Arabs want peace. Listen to what Abdel Khaleq Hassuna and Michel 'Aflak are saying, but Israel has to change its policy. Not to go in the way of imperialism, to get closer to them, to understand them".

What in effect are they proposing to us? Bandung? The 29th of November? "Peace this" and "peace that", they say. We respond. To their credit I can say that they did not try to flatter.

After the reading of the poems there was no point in mincing words. But they are completely lacking in any feeling of guilt. They feel that injustice has been done to them, that their rights were trampled; they are not pedantic about the subtleties of poetry. They are the "mouthpiece of the people". No, they do not feel any guilt. They have eradicated from their memory the night of the invasion. They are part of the Arab world, but they bear no responsibility for the big attack. They were crushed. Their land was taken. Their world was destroyed . . .

After ten years we met face to face, in a room between four walls. How to compromise between two awesome loves? Between two national movements?

Most of them understand the language. One, Hanna Abu-Hanna, speaks an amazing Hebrew, slow, but measured. But even more impressive is the elderly Jabra Nicola. Avot Yeshurun swears that Jabra must have read *Ha'melitz*.[3] Gaunt and tight-jawed. He smiles, but it is difficult to decipher his smile. When he speaks Hebrew, without any foreign traces whatsoever, he accuses Shamir of speaking down to them. "It is hard to find an Arabic speaker among you", he says, "Yes, I knew Hebrew even when we were the *majority* here". After that he speaks against art in service of the nation. The conver-

3 *Ha'melitz* was a Hebrew literary journal that appeared in Russia between 1860 and 1904. Its language reflected an ornate pre-modern Hebrew.

sation touches on everything. Rashid Hussein serves coffee with cardamom.

One of them limps. Rests on his cane, says he must go. His friends explain that he must go before the curfew. We are dumbfounded. It is easier to deal with abstract matters.

In the meantime it has gotten late. People are repeating what has already been said. I do not deny it: I too, the undersigned, was also a little bit moved. At one moment the meeting seems to me like an absurd adventure, like a dream. At the next moment it seems there is nothing more humane, fundamental, touching, than this meeting. Why did we have to wait ten years?

For certain. We did not solve anything. The hour is late. But ours was a conversation interrupted. Stumbling and getting up, groping, without flattery and without lies.

We will meet again with the first rainfall of winter, on their turf. This time they will be the hosts and we will make our claims. We have what to say.

We disperse. Later, crowded in a car crossing the night in the wee hours, we ask ourselves several questions for which we have not yet found answers.

Even though there were no further meetings of the group as planned, many friendly encounters took place in Tel Aviv, Nazareth and several other places in which Jewish and Arab writers participated, and to which I was often invited. As a rule, in these events good camaraderie was displayed by all. The Palestinian citizens of Israel exhibited, in recent decades, an excellent command of Hebrew, whereas their Jewish counterparts did not acquire a real knowledge of Arabic. The discussions were therefore conducted in Hebrew, and there was still a need to translate the relevant texts. However none of these later encounters was as shocking as the one convened in 1958 by Rashid Hussein and Benjamin Tammuz.

CHAPTER

8

FATHER

A great dream that inspired me from the moment of my arrival in Israel (and indeed even before that), namely to study at the Hebrew University, kept getting postponed, kept slipping away. At first I was immersed in my Hebrew language studies, and after that, thirty months of military service. After my discharge from the army I worked as a junior bank clerk in order to help support my family. What should have been the most temporary of jobs went on for four years. Finally I planned to move to Jerusalem to attend the 1956 school year, but the sudden death of my father forced me to continue working at the bank for another three years. Only the actual establishment of Tel Aviv University in 1957 enabled me to study without moving to another city, and in fact, without leaving my job at the bank, at least for a year or two, as will be told in this chapter.

My father was a clerk in a British bank in Iraq, where he worked for some thirty consecutive years. When he arrived in Israel he found a job at the Tel Aviv Bank where they were seeking an experienced bank clerk like himself, in particular since the department that hired him dealt in international credit, a branch in which my father had specialized back in Baghdad. It was a relatively comfortable position, and he was lucky, considering that many of the immigrants from Iraq who had worked desk jobs, now had to undertake physical labor in agriculture or in factories. Not only were such jobs physically taxing for the adult immigrants who were accustomed to clerical work; but the very fact of the physical labor seemed to them unsuitable for well-educated men. My father was pleased not to share the fate of those whose self-esteem suffered, whether due to the "humiliating" jobs they had to accept, or because they joined the ranks of the unemployed who returned home day after day from the employment bureau with fallen faces, disappointing their families who awaited better days to come. The middle class suffered more humiliation and disappointment than any other class. My father was spared this fate, and of this he was most certainly aware. From time to time he would come home and tell about an old friend whom he knew from back in Baghdad, an educated person who had been in a managerial position, but had to accept a job in construction or in the Public Works Authority, which mainly entailed paving and maintaining roads.

But the bank my father worked for in Israel was not like the bank in Baghdad, where most of the work was conducted in English (including the contact with the British managers) and conversations with the Bank's clients, many of whom were Jews, took place in Judeo-Arabic or in Arabic. Things were different in Israel. My father knew very little Hebrew upon his arrival (in his childhood they were still taught basic Hebrew reading and Bible in the lower classes at school); but like many of those who arrived in Israel with "Iraqi" Hebrew, he found little resemblance between what he had learned in his childhood and what he heard and read in Israel. Two or three months after arriving in Israel, he was sent by the Jewish Agency to a boarding school to study Hebrew for beginners, not far from Ra'anana where we were living temporarily. He stayed there for two or three months but when he returned to the Ra'anana Transit Camp, he realized how limited his progress in Hebrew had been. He would never be able to read a Hebrew newspaper or book, and his Hebrew speech was utterly inarticulate. What's more, the Middle Eastern accent he brought with him was then considered inferior and uncouth. Therefore he did his best to speak in English with the veteran Israelis as with European immigrants, but to his disappointment, these had little knowledge of the English language. At his new bank he could handle the written material, given that many of the banking terms were still in English, or something akin to English, as the State of Israel had only recently been released from British Imperial rule (it was between 1952 and 1956 that my father worked at the bank), however his contact with clients in Israel was problematic. Not everyone knew English well and my father felt like a helpless foreigner during these interactions. He was a reticent person (one could say that he was introverted) and only seldom did I hear him complain about the hardships he encountered at work day in and day out. While I, along with my older sister and younger brother, made progress in our knowledge of Hebrew – both spoken and written – at a rather reasonable pace, father, who was born in 1900, faltered and stumbled every step of the way. Occasionally he would ask me grammatical questions (I was then the family "linguist"), and every time I tried to give him an answer based on his knowledge of Arabic, a cognate language, I was astounded to discover that his knowledge of classical Arabic (*Fusha*, which is mainly the written language and that of radio broadcasts) was quite meager. He had worked for over thirty years to adopt English as his primary language, and as such he neglected what he had learned of Arabic in his youth. My father never read an Arabic newspaper (in Iraq he would make do with reading the English daily *Baghdad Times*), and I never saw him reading an Arabic book, although he loved books. When a poem of mine appeared for the first time in a Baghdad newspaper (a prose poem entitled *Spark*), I showed my father the printed poem and he tried to read it, finally lifting his head to me and saying: "Maybe you can explain to me the meaning of this piece? Not all the words are clear to me, not even the title "Spark" (*qabas* in Arabic) is familiar to me." Of course, it was not only his estrangement from classical Arabic that brought about this misunderstanding, but primarily his distance from the world of poetry and the concepts of modern "literary" poetry (as opposed to sung poetry, which has different conventions). Therefore, in Israel, too, it was hard for me to explain Hebrew linguistic phenomena to father because of his weak knowledge of the basics of Arabic (I would venture to say that the members of my generation, who were generally well-versed in literary Arabic and its grammar, learned Hebrew with relative ease).

Father was not a healthy man. At the age of forty, still in Baghdad, he was diagnosed with acute diabetes. For a few years he followed a strict diet. But his arrival in Israel wreaked havoc when it came to cautious eating; during our first years in Israel we ate "Agency food" (i.e., provided by the Jewish Agency), neither that nor the strict rationing practiced in those days (courtesy of Dov Yosef, Ben-Gurion's Minister of Rationing) boded well for his diet. My father didn't complain of any health problems, and I don't remember him making even periodic doctor's visits during most of his years in Israel. One Friday, my father returned from work and happily announced to my mother that he was going on a two-week vacation beginning that coming Sunday, and that he was considering going to a convalescent home to finally get some rest. We ate lunch all together (on that day even my brother Henry was home on furlough from his army unit, so we were in full family forum at that meal). After that we all went to rest. Suddenly I heard a terrifying grunt come from my parents' bedroom. I jumped up and ran to his room, and I heard him saying that he was having trouble breathing. Those were his last words. I ran in a frenzy to the house of Dr. Alcalay, a neighbor who was a doctor and a family friend, and dragged him with me in the middle of his lunch. When we got back to our apartment I could hear bitter weeping and I recognized the voices of my mother and my grand-mother, my mother's mother, who lived with us at the time. Dr. Alcalay checked my father and said: "There's practically no pulse. His chances of survival are very slim!" I knew then that that was it, and that the doctor had used those words only so as not to utter the word "death"; and so the decree was irrevocable. We called an ambulance and traveled from our Ramat Gan apartment to Beilinson Hospital in Petah Tikva, where my father was pronounced dead. The autopsy revealed blockage in the aorta as the main cause of death, probably as a result of his diabetes. We returned home feeling like victims of an inconceivable ruse. Just two or three hours ago father had been completely fine, and now he was dead. We were fatherless now. The next morning my grandmother, who shared my room, told me that I had called out in my sleep several times, "How could this have happened?" My mother made do the following day with one sentence, a sentence I remember well: "We no longer have a father". My mother, who was forty-seven years old at the time, turned out to be a strong person. At the end of the mourning period she put on a façade of "business as usual". She cried when she was alone, but I didn't hear her wailing or protesting to heaven and earth about being widowed at such a young age. She was an educated and attractive woman, but in the years following my father's death she never even considered remarrying. My father was her cousin, her lover, and her friend, and all through her married life she considered herself responsible for the comfort and happiness of her husband. She always considered her own comfort as secondary.

My father's death caused a great upheaval in my family's life. His salary from the bank stopped coming in, and since he was relatively new on the job, my family did not receive any financial compensa-tion. My sister and I were working then. But my sister was at an age at which her classmates from the Alliance school in Baghdad were beginning to get married and have children; as for me – my dream of moving to Jerusalem and studying there had just been shattered. The seven-day mourning period for my father, at the end of 1956, coincided with the discussions of Israel's withdrawal from the Sinai and from Sharm al-Sheikh, which it had conquered during the 1956 war (which we called the "Sinai Campaign" and which the Arabs referred to as the "Tripartite [British French Israeli] Aggression"). Our many conversations during condolence calls became unbearable for me. We did not pay a heavy price for that war, but Israel's reputation and the appreciation it had earned in many places in the world severely declined. Now Israel appeared as a state with a conquering army (and we called it the Israel *Defense* Forces) that chose collaboration with the declining imperial powers over the possibility of rapprochement with the Arab world that surrounds it from all sides. In addition, Ben-Gurion eventually had to return all the territory captured in the war to Egypt – due to pressure from the two superpowers – in exchange for a vague promise of access to Egyptian territorial waters.

Only because I wished to maintain a minimum of politeness did I not argue with the guests at our house during those difficult days. It was clear to me that we had moved farther away from the possibility of a peace agreement with our neighbors, and at the same time we had turned Nasser, whom we called in those days the "Egyptian tyrant", into the great hero of the Arab world and the leader of the Third World. He used his great political savvy to turn the failures of the Egyptian armies into a springboard for great political success.

9

HIGHER LEARNING IN LOWER TEL AVIV

In 1957 a small university opened in Tel Aviv, Israel's largest city. The university was temporarily housed in vacant buildings around Abu Kabir, near Jaffa, on the southern edge of the city. My dream of moving to Jerusalem to study at the Hebrew University had been set aside, since I still had to work in order to help support my family. If I studied and lived in Jerusalem, my family would not only have to support me, but also forgo the salary I received from my job at the bank.

Naturally I was very pleased about the opening of a university nearby, despite the fact that the university didn't have great luminaries or impressive academic names as Martin Buber, Gershom Scholem, S.D. Goitein, or Yehezkel Kaufman. Indeed, the lay-out of the new university was far from what I had imagined a proper university campus to be; and furthermore the new institution did not initially have a suitable university library. I soon realized that the absence of those academic giants from the faculty was not necessarily a flaw, since many of the teachers who taught us in Tel Aviv were young and energetic scholars (many of them had studied or taught in Jerusalem), and their enthusiasm was often a blessing for a student just starting out.

They did not set up a department in every academic discipline, and certainly not in the subjects I wanted to study, such as Arabic language and linguistics, so I had to focus on Hebrew studies. During my first year I minored in Bible and Hebrew literature, while majoring in Jewish history. From my second year onwards I chose a second major – Hebrew language – instead of the two minors. I found my fortune in the new department, and after three years was chosen to be a junior teacher there. During these years I received a solid foundation in many fields of Jewish studies, which until then had been virtually foreign to me. In Jewish history I focused on the Second Temple period (under the aforementioned Joshua Efron, a solid scholar of Talmudic and Christian historical sources) and on the Jews of Muslim lands and in the Ottoman Empire (under Zvi Ankori, also mentioned, a rousing lecturer and truly impressive scholar).

Among my most memorable teachers from my first years of study was the Talmud professor, Dr. Binyamin de Vries, a thick-bearded Orthodox Dutch Jew with whom we studied Tractate Pesahim inside-out. I was enthused by his progressive teaching methods and modern scholarly discourse. It was different from that of a traditional yeshiva student, as it used the terminology of contemporary humanities and social sciences scholarship: harmonization, documentation, etc. And since this was my first exposure to the Talmud, de Vries helped me relate to the Talmudic text and to speak in contemporary terms about events and concepts of the distant past. Another teacher, Professor Menachem Haran, taught a first-year course focusing on the Book of Numbers. For me, his class was like "Bible 101", a general introduction to the problems faced by biblical commentators and scholars in the Middle Ages and in the present.

In the last two years of my studies, my passions shifted from the field of Hebrew literature to language. I found my home in the Department of Hebrew Language (in Tel Aviv and later in Jerusalem) for ten years, until the mid-sixties when I made the transition into modern Arabic literature. In the courses I took in the Hebrew language department, I discovered the similarities between Arabic, my mother tongue, and Hebrew, my adopted language – a proximity that for me intensified from day to day. The introductory courses in the Semitic languages were particularly exciting, since I arrived with a series of superficial ideas and misconceptions that I had amassed regarding the history of these languages. From a very young age I believed that Arabic was THE Semitic language from which all the other languages derived, in part since the "case" system existed fully in Arabic, while in the other Semitic languages it had mostly disappeared. And now, along came linguists who explained that the linguistic families do not have one mother-tongue (for example: Latin, as we know it, is not the "mother" of the romance languages), and that it is not possible to say that language A came out of language B, but rather that geographic proximity over the course of thousands of years produced linguistic families, even if each language has its own characteristics.

In the field of Hebrew language itself, the courses I took on post-Biblical Hebrew (that of the Second Temple Period) liberated me from my preconception of it as a "religious" language, limited to the Jewish sages. While I had assumed that it was not open to the languages and cultures of the ancient world, now I was beginning to understand that this language was generally receptive to a large degree of lexical borrowing, in particular from Greek, and that the contact in the Second Temple Period – one of the most "religious" periods in Jewish history – between the Jews and other peoples was not negligible at all. And lo and behold, many of the terms for religious concepts and institutions in the so-called "language of the Sages" are borrowed from Greek. Here is an example: the word "Sanhedrin", referring to the supreme religious and juridical council in Second Temple Period Jewish society, comes from the Greek word meaning a sort of "house of elders" (the syllable "san" at the beginning of the word is related to the English word "senate" or the medical term "senility"). Of course the discovery of such scientific facts regarding Arabic and Hebrew did not alter my love for either of them, but taught me that they are normal languages with a dynamic linguistic history, and that they are, as such, not different from the rest of the languages of the world.

So as not to digress into this linguistic-historical discussion, which captivates me to this day, I will proceed to talk about the teachers who gave me my foundation in the grammar and history of the Hebrew language. Among the great scholars who taught me in those years was Professor Yehosua Blau, a pre-eminent scholar of written Judeo-Arabic. At Tel Aviv University he masterfully taught the theory of Hebrew phonology and morphology. In his course entitled "Linguistic Analysis of Biblical Texts", Blau would select a few verses from a biblical text (for example, Genesis I) and, over the course of an entire year, put all of his knowledge into analyzing it backwards and forwards on all of its etymological, morphological, and semantic levels, citing from the theories of scholars and linguists. At the end of one year like this, I felt that my knowledge of the Hebrew language had been vastly transformed toward a historical and contemporary understanding. Another teacher was the late Professor Shelomo Morag, then a young man, grand in stature and with an impressive accent and voice. Morag taught an introduction to Semitic languages, and I also took his course on the Hebrew linguistic traditions of the various Jewish communities, in particular concerning the pronunciation of post-Biblical Hebrew. The German-born Professor Eli Eitan, my future colleague at the secretariat of the Academy for Hebrew Language, taught a seminar on the development of words and terminologies in Modern Hebrew. I recall that he advised me on a seminar paper I wrote on poet Yonathan Ratosh's solution to the problem of the translation of linguistic context in the Hebrew translation of George Bernard Shaw's *Pygmalion*. *Pygmalion* is a play known for its "linguistic" content: how a professor of English language decides to teach the simple flower girl aristocratic English. Ratosh's translation attempted to bridge a series of difficult socio-linguistic gaps between Hebrew and English, and not always successfully, as it is indeed an impossible mission. I should add that, in his introduction to the Hebrew translation, Ratosh remarks that the great difficulty faced by the translator is that while good English is spoken by the aristocracy and street English, or Cockney, is spoken by the simple people, in Hebrew the situation is the reverse. According to Ratosh, the simple people (those coming from the Arab world, or some of them) speak a correct and superior Hebrew (meaning they pronounce the gutturals, etc.) while the "upper classes" (e.g., Ashkenazim, kibbutz members, etc.) speak a flawed Hebrew. I understand Ratosh's problems in terms of translating *Pygmalion*, but in his general characterization of the situation of Modern Hebrew he makes generalizations that no linguist can agree with since the level and quality of language are not only dependent on the pronunciation of the consonants, but also on linguistic culture, intonation, and lexical wealth. Thus on this point I must differ with the generalizations of the well-known poet-translator.

To return to my studies in the Department of Hebrew Language in Tel Aviv: during these years I developed a special relationship with some of the most important Hebrew linguists, many of whom were at the beginning or in the middle of their academic careers at the time. This was made possible by the relatively small number of students in the department (when I enrolled in the university in 1958 there were about 100 students; in the year 2000 there were over 25,000; and today it has the largest student body of any Israeli university) and the fact that we were older than the students in Jerusalem (I started my studies there at age 26, about five years late, but in my case, and that of some of classmates in Abu Kabir, this delay only heightened my eager absorption of every word and idea that the young professors would utter in their lessons). In the 1959–60 school year, Tel Aviv University's temporary building underwent a general renovation, and classes were transferred to an elementary school near Allenby Street in the center of Tel Aviv. Many of the older students at the university (and there were many in those days) had a hard time sitting on the miniature chairs, which were occupied by small school-children in the morning hours. The following year we returned to the original campus (if one can call the small complex a campus).

My excitement at studying Hebrew linguistics was so great that, as I wrote earlier, I decided to start writing a linguistic column in the literary supplement of *Kol Ha-Am*. I called the column "Questions on Language", in which for nearly three years I discussed issues about language that arose in Israeli society, and also answered readers' questions and caveats. I signed the column under a pseudonym, Dan Tirosh, fearing that the publication of my name as a columnist in the Communist Party newspaper would make it difficult for me to find a job. However, to my great surprise, some of those in charge of the language department and a few of the members of the scientific secretariat of the Academy of Hebrew Language, discovered the true identity of the writer and even took my column into consideration when discussing and approving my employment at the secretariat of the Academy in 1962.

Several years later, after my return from my doctoral studies in England, and in my first years as a teacher at the Hebrew Department at Tel Aviv University, I agreed to write a similar column in *Massa* (the literary supplement of the daily, *La-Merhav*, which was eventually taken over, along with the newspaper itself, by *Davar*). This new column was called "On the Tip of the Tongue", and it, too, ran for about three years (the column was the initiative of my friend Menahem Brinker, who edited *Massa* for some time).

In 1961, I took my final exams in the Hebrew Language Department, and graduated with honors. I took great pleasure in this, since in the past (in particular at the Shammash High School in

Baghdad), I had generally gotten mediocre grades, as my interest in schoolwork per se was much weaker than my literary writing endeavors, as far back as my last years in high school. And now the studies themselves had taken center stage.

A few possibilities now presented themselves: teaching high school, or working as a copy-editor at one of the newspapers or publishing houses. But ultimately I did not have to choose between either of these. A short time after completing my studies, Tel Aviv University offered me a part-time position as an instructor in the Hebrew language department (teaching Arabic vocalization, composition, and grammar to the students of the department). A year or two later I was taken on as a member of the scientific secretariat of the Academy of Hebrew Language in Jerusalem, as I shall explain in the following chapter. In 1964, the first buildings of the new Ramat Aviv campus, in north Tel Aviv, were completed, and I was one of the teachers who taught there on the opening day of the Gilman Building for Humanities. A year later I received a scholarship from the British Council to study in England, and I left for London along with Terrie, now my wife.

Abu Kabir is where I began my academic life, reading books that perhaps I wouldn't have read had I not studied there. I read Gershom Scholem's book *Sabbatai Sevi and the Sabbatean Movement in his Lifetime* as part of my studies in the Jewish History Department. I devoured it, and for many weeks I remained under the spell created by Professor Scholem around an historical figure and event that were otherwise not part of my personal arsenal. I was thrilled by his descriptions of the historical aspiration for messianic redemption, which captivated many of the Jewish communities in the seventeenth century. And above all, this book impressed me because of the use it made of secondary sources, from which the great scholar gleaned some of his astonishing new knowledge in the field of Jewish mysticism. Some of these sources had been considered in the past to be rubbish and not worthy of review. As for me, I now believe that my encounter with this book sparked my scholarly urge and encouraged me to seek out an academic career in the coming years.

The setting up of Tel Aviv University was, therefore, the beginning of my passion for scholarship and scholars. Furthermore, I managed to convince some of my best friends from Maki to study at the university in Abu Kabir, friends who were also on the brink of giving up on academic studies. Among them I will mention my good friend Michael Harsegor, once the literary editor of *Kol Ha'am* and later a professor of European History; he continued his studies at the Sorbonne after completing his studies at Tel Aviv. Another such friend was the late Binyamin Cohen, who, along with his wife, the painter Ruth Schloss, was one of my closest friends from my days in the Party. I led Binyamin to the registration office in Abu Kabir and "forced" him to enroll. Binyamin was an excellent student who became a professor in Greek and Roman history and published important articles in international periodicals in the field. A third friend, who had already enrolled at the University a year before I did, was Yaakov Shai Shavit, who published his poetry in the literary supplement of *Kol Ha'am* just as I did. Yaakov was and remains a close friend. After completing his studies at the university he worked for over thirty years as a high school history and language teacher. Happily, Yaakov returned to writing poetry after his retirement, and since the 1990s has published five collections of his new poetry.

If one were to ask me what were my happiest years at Tel Aviv University, I would answer, without hesitating: those first days at Abu Kabir. There I was surrounded by a group of students, many of them not so young, who were enthusiastic about studying and who, just like me, yearned to enter the gates of learning and research. In the Department of Hebrew Language I befriended a group of students who were ardent lovers of the Hebrew language. We began to study in Tel Aviv and, around 1958, after completing our Bachelor's Degrees, we went to Jerusalem to do a Master's Degree in the Department of Hebrew Language at the Hebrew University. In us the teachers there encountered a close-knit group of students with a great desire to learn, and this bolstered the reputation of Tel Aviv University (which many did not take seriously in those years). We eagerly participated in the seminars of the senior professors there – Ben Haim, Kutscher, Rabin, and others – and indeed we proved, to ourselves and to others, that what we had learned at the new university in Tel Aviv indeed reflected new directions in the study of Hebrew language. We were like dreamers, and sometimes like drunks, as we were fortunate enough to study with the luminaries of the "Jerusalem School" of Hebrew studies. They treated us well, but none of us could forget Abu Kabir where we found our first academic home.

CHAPTER

10

ROMAN À CLEF: THREE YEARS AT THE ACADEMY OF THE HEBREW LANGUAGE

On March 6, 1963, about two years after completing my studies at Tel Aviv University, I received in the mail a letter from the Academy of the Hebrew Language in Jerusalem, which included the following sentence:

> The administration of the Academy of the Hebrew Language, in its meeting of March 1, 1963, has decided to invite you to work at the scientific secretariat for a period of 6 months . . .

The letter was signed by the administrative director of the Academy. My surprise at receiving this letter was great, since I still saw myself as a novice in the field of Hebrew language, and to a large extent a "new immigrant". And even if I had made good in the Hebrew Language Department at Abu Kabir, the very name "Academy" – whose forerunner, the Hebrew Language Committee, was founded by the legendary Eliezer Ben Yehuda, the reviver of Modern Hebrew – rang sublime and remote in the ears of a young man who had just ten years earlier arrived in Israel without knowing a word of the language.

Several weeks earlier I had seen an advertisement in the newspaper announcing an opening for a position on the secretariat of the Academy in Jerusalem. The ad said that it was desirable for the applicant to hold a PhD in Hebrew language. I hesitated, and in the end I addressed a letter to the Academy, although I was only in the middle of my Master's Degree and far from the required title of "Doctor"; I assumed that my chances to get the position were slim, but no harm could be done by sending in an application. I would not be surprised if they weren't interested. To my surprise I received a reply designating a time for an interview. And then the unexpected happened: I got the position. In those days I still lived in Ramat Gan with my mother; I travelled by bus to my classes in Jerusalem and spent time on the wonderful Givat Ram campus two or three days a week. I had already quit my job at the bank and had received a scholarship that covered my tuition. When I began working at the Academy I had to move to Jerusalem and only returned home to Ramat Gan on weekends. In Jerusalem I rented a room in the apartment of a long-retired veteran journalist. The apartment was located in an alley in the center of town (following the journalist's death, a short time after I stopped living there, the alley was named after him). He was pleased to hear that I was working at the Hebrew Language Academy, and told me about his long acquaintance with Eliezer Ben Yehuda and with several famous members of the Hebrew Language Committee such as Silman, Zuta, and Lupschitz. He had also met Bialik, the great Hebrew poet, during the 1930s. He was a widower and his circle of friends was very small. For this reason he sought out company, and he was very disappointed that I did not spend weekends with him.

I worked at the Academy for about three years – some of the happiest years of my life. Here I was, dealing with linguistic topics from morning to evening, and for this work I was actually paid a salary! I had become accustomed to making a living from work that I didn't love and doing the things I loved in my spare time – without pay, and sometimes even paying tuition or entrance fees to lectures. But the greatest part of the experience for me was the simple fact of working in the company of such giants as Professors Tur-Sinai, Ben-Haim, Polotzky, Kutscher, Sadan; and being colleagues with the excellent linguists who served on the secretariat of the Academy and on the editorial board of the historical dictionary that was compiled under its auspices. Tur-Sinai, the president of the Academy, would invite me for conversations in his spacious office and tell me about his research of the Bible (his great work was called *The Hebrew Language and the Old Testament*), while Meir Madan, the veteran scientific secretary, who was an observant Jew from a totally religious world, surprised me when he was not shocked at my very secular, even Marxist, approach to the Hebrew language – which was for him the Holy Language – and to the current situation of the Jewish people.

He accepted me as I was, and did not make any attempt to "Judaize" me, and for that I was very grateful.

Yet, among all the people I met during my work at the Academy, I particularly esteemed and was fond of Professor Ze'ev Ben-Haim, vice-president of the Academy, and later its president. Ben-Haim was one of my favorite teachers from the day I began studying at the Hebrew University. His seminars in Aramaic as well as Samaritan Hebrew – of the community that lived uninterruptedly in the Holy Land since ancient times – riveted me. Other of his seminars, such as "Readings in Medieval Hebrew Grammarians", surprised me in their erudition and originality. Upon joining the staff of the Academy, I discovered that this innovativeness was characteristic of all his books and articles. This man, who spent much of his time hunched over ancient documents, turned out to be skilled in modern work methods and advanced technology. It was he who pushed for the "mechanization" (the word for "computerization" didn't yet exist in Hebrew) of the preparation of the Historical Dictionary of the Hebrew Language, a labor of love that he was in charge of for half a century. He understood from the very beginning that the preparation of a full historical dictionary would take many, many decades; therefore he preferred to avoid preparing the material manually, but rather to use electronic storage – not only to preserve the material, but to give the linguistic researcher an important temporary database, years before the completion of the work. And another act of daring by Ben-Haim: he was the one who proposed to add to the Hebrew alphabet two additional letters, one signifying the vowel **a** and the other for the vowel **e**. The lack of distinct letters for these vowels in Hebrew – as opposed to the diacritical signs that are used to denote the vowel sounds – resulted in a great gap between what we write and what we are meant to decode and to read. I do not wish to dwell on the details of his proposal and its incarnations in the institutions of the Academy up until its ultimate failure, and I mention it only to illustrate the remarkable boldness of this man. Who better than he knew that the Hebrew elites would balk at such a proposal to change Hebrew orthography and the form of the Hebrew word as we had inherited it from our ancient forefathers? In a private conversation, Ben-Haim confessed to me that he never believed he would be able to pass this proposal at the Academy or among the public; but nonetheless he invested days and nights in preparing the proposal and the discussion of it, so that the issue of the Hebrew alphabet would remain on the agenda.

Besides the friendships and contacts I made while working at the Academy offices, my main job was to coordinate several of the committees that dealt with terminology. These committees were made up of linguists, members of the Academy, and experts in different fields, such as technology, geography, woodworking, construction, etc. Until recently there were almost no Hebrew words in use in these professions, and the professionals themselves used foreign, often unfamiliar, words. Each professional committee would assemble several times over the course of a year or two (and sometimes more than that) to go over the list of professional terms. Some of the new words came from post-Biblical Hebrew sources; but often members of the committee would propose a Hebrew neologism made of the typical three-letter root in its different morphemes. Of course, members of the committees preferred the first method, namely, searching in the sources – but in many cases they had to make do with the invention method. And in any case, many if not most of the Academy's new words were rejected by workers in the field, even after their acceptance and publication in professional dictionaries. Sometimes I felt that our work was Sisyphean, even if indispensable.

On these professional committees, I had the privilege of meeting in person with some of the leading linguists and scholars of the various professions. Among these I met Dr. A. Brauer, the geographer and essayist who wrote in *Ha'aretz* for decades (he was the father of another geographer, Dr. Moshe Brauer – my colleague at Tel Aviv University, who served as dean of the faculty when I worked there). A member of another committee whose memory is etched in my mind is the poet and famous literary translator, Avraham Shlonsky. Shlonsky was a member of the Academy, and in this capacity he participated in the discussions of the committee on zoological terms, whose meetings actually took place in Tel Aviv, and in which I occasionally participated. My admiration for Shlonsky dated back to my first years in Israel, but now that I had tasted his spontaneous work style, which was based on great linguistic knowledge, my admiration for him grew sevenfold. He was too busy to attend committee meetings regularly, and indeed he missed many meetings, much to my disappointment. But the moment he would sit with us his uniqueness was apparent. Although Shlonsky did not grow up as a Torah scholar in the traditional sense, his knowledge of Talmudic literature amazed us every time he participated in the discussion. When we had given up on the prospect of finding a Hebrew word for an animal or a fish, we would turn to the illustrious poet, and he would scratch the bald spot on top of his head surrounded by two clumps of white hair, and suddenly bring, out of the depths of his memory, a mishnaic or talmudic name from the days of the Second Temple or later.

As already noted, I had admired Shlonsky and his Shlonskian language for several years before meeting him personally. I always loved his poetry, and even more than that I loved his translations from Russian poetry such as "Eugene Onegin" [as it is usually called in English] in its different versions, an anthology of Russian poetry, and Shakespeare's *Hamlet*. And most of all I loved his translation of the novel *Colas Breugnon* by the French writer Romain Rolland. I read this translation even before I was familiar enough with the subtleties of the Hebrew language, and had to resort to the dictionary a lot while reading. But in subsequent years I returned to read the book; Shlonsky's linguistic ruses may have distanced it from its original form, but they turned it into an amazing Hebrew work – exciting, and surprising in its innovativeness.

I would also meet Shlonsky from time to time in literary circles, in particular at his favorite club, Tzavta (meaning "being together", which Shlonsky himself named), and also in meetings of the Israeli Peace Committee, of which he was a longtime activist. Throughout the 1960s I tried not to miss an opportunity to catch Shlonsky lecturing or reading his poetry.

Although we were not close friends, he did recognize me, and at meetings of the zoological terms committee he would address me as "my young friend". My last encounter with him was in the spring of 1973, a short time before he died. I arrived on a Friday at the office building where the Sifriyat Poalim (Worker's Library) publishing house was located (above the bookshop of the publishing house on Allenby Street in Tel Aviv). The purpose of my visit: to read proofs of the book *Butterfly River*, which I was publishing there – a selection of modern Syrian and Lebanese poetry that I had translated into Hebrew. Shlonsky, who for years was the godfather of this publication house, no longer had any official role but he visited the offices from time to time. When he saw me seated by one of the tables, he approached me and said: "Show us your wares, Somekh". He was not particularly impressed by the combination "Syrian and Lebanese poetry", but nonetheless he picked up one of the proof pages I was working on, and immediately his eyes captured a mistake in one of the diacritical signs. He brought it to my attention and went on his way. Several days later I read that he had died, and so that correction was one of Shlonsky's last "literary" acts (because of his great love of language, there were those who called him "Lashonsky", a play on the Hebrew word for "language", *lashon*).

I also had some contact with the writer and Nobel Prize laureate, S.Y. Agnon, during my years at the Academy. I had the task of calling his house a day or two prior to each plenary session in which he was supposed to participate. He or his wife would avoid giving an explicit answer to the question, "Will he be attending?", and indeed most meetings were not graced by his presence. These sessions of the Academy were the institution's final decision-making forum, during which its members would accept or reject the lists that were prepared by the terminology committees and discuss decisions of the administrative committees about the Academy's budget. The secretaries of the terminology committees would send the new lists to the members of the assembly ahead of time so that they could look them over, but in most cases members would come to the meetings without having prepared ahead of time. During discussion time, some of these members would browse through the duplicated pages and occasionally one of them would ask to speak. The comments of members of the assembly were important and sometimes enlightening, but not always the result of careful review of the pages. On occasion a particular word would bother one of the members for reasons that were beside the point, and he would expound upon it in order to liberate himself from a personal problem. At one such meeting, discussion revolved around the lists of the committee on library terminology, whose work I had coordinated for nearly three years. At this meeting Agnon himself was there. All of a sudden, Agnon raised his hand in the course of the discussion. He stood up in his place and announced that he would like to talk about the term *roman mafte'ah* (the Hebrew equivalent of the French *Roman à clef* (literally, "novel with a key", referring to a novel in whose fictional characters one can identify real-life personalities of the time). Surprised, we waited to hear what he had to say. Well, it turned out that he had seized the opportunity to clear up a misunderstanding (and perhaps also settle scores) that had arisen following the appearance of his latest book, *Shira* (1971). Following is the translation of his speech as it was recorded in the protocol of the meeting, which appeared in the *Protocols of the Academy of the Hebrew Language*:

> Heaven forbid that I should write "novels with a key". If there be all sorts of people who are attributed to the people in my story – let them be. Once, on an autumn evening, I was strolling in the streets of Jerusalem. A woman chanced upon me and asked me, do I still reside in Beit HaKerem? I told her, never have I resided in Beit HaKerem. She said to me, and where does my lord reside? I wanted to come pay him a visit. I told her, for what? She answered, saying, but my lord wrote about my father. I asked her who her father was, and where had I mentioned her father? She said to me, in his story "Two Torah Scholars Who Were in our Town". My lord did not call my father by name, but it is my father. I told her, since I do not know who you are, how can I know who your father is?
>
> A year or two later I went to a certain physician to wish him a happy birthday. The doctor presented me to his guests, and among them was that same lady who told me that I had written about her father. Said the woman to the doctor and all those gathered, we know one another, for he wrote about my father.
>
> That is one tale, and here is another.
>
> A few months ago a couple from America – a man and his wife – came to visit me. He, a doctor, and she, the daughter of a Torah scholar from the Horowitz-Halevy family, whom I knew in my youth in my native city. Among the things the woman said was, after all, my lord knew my father and even wrote about him in his story "Two Torah Scholars". I said to her, I knew your father, and his name is Horowitz like the name of my protagonist, but I was not referring to her father.
>
> Just as there are people who attach their acquaintances to the people in my stories, so are there people who are identified by admirers and nemeses alike, as if they were written in my books. In the end, after one says to such a person, I saw what Agnon wrote about you, he begins to see himself in light of that same character who is written in my book. In order not to delay the negotiations about the terminology that will be discussed today, I will be brief and say, never have I intended to conceive in my stories a character

about whom it can be said, the author is referring to so-and-so; a true storyteller makes a pact that every soul he creates in his story is a living soul. But since there are all sorts of know-it-alls who see themselves as if they know everything, as if nothing is hidden from them, we are likely to hear from them that the soul we created was chosen from him in this world, as if they knew them even before we had the thought of giving them life.

There is no need to add that my inclusion of this excerpt here is not intended to shed light on the book *Shira* or on any particular literary term; it is to say that Agnon's presence at this meeting was for me an extraordinary experience. His unique accent, his typically Ashkenazi Hebrew, gave his words a tune without which the words would not have been so Agnon-esque on that day.

In the summer of 1965 I requested a one-year leave from the Academy, during which I would travel to London to study general linguistics at the University of London. I won a scholarship from the British Council, and as a student of British culture from as far back as my high school days in Baghdad, I could not resist the temptation that the scholarship presented. I would go away for a year and expand my knowledge in the field of general linguistics, I said to myself. I would return at the end of a year to my present work, which I so loved. The truth is that besides the charms of London, there were two more reasons that inclined me toward taking the trip. Two of my great teachers, Professor Zeev Ben-Haim and Professor Yehezkel Kutscher, each proposed to me, respectively and on their own personal initiative, topics for a doctorate for which I would be competent after completing my Master's Degree. With these two proposals before me, it seemed to me that I would do best to put off the decision for a year and as such also avoid being trapped between two lions! Ben-Haim's proposal was to deal with the glosses providing the meaning of Hebrew talmudic terms from the field of agriculture and labor in the commentary of the tenth-century Jewish theologian, Hai Gaon, as they appeared in his commentary on the Mishna. Kutscher, for his part, suggested I try to clarify the scope and meaning of Hebrew and Aramaic words that survived until our day in the Arabic language of the Galilee. Both of these subjects, as attractive as they were, did not meet my heart's desire. Both subjects dealt with the Mishnaic Hebrew of the Jewish sages, which was at the center of these two eminent scholars' worlds. While at the center of my world was the contemporary Hebrew language and the dynamics of Hebrew revival in our day.

And the second reason: I was about to wed my girlfriend Terrie, who had come from the United States, and she was thrilled at the prospect of spending the first year of our married life in the legendary London!

CHAPTER
11

A FAMILY OF MY OWN

Sometime in 1964 I got the urge to go on a trip in Europe. I had worked full time, for the two years leading up to that, at the Academy of the Hebrew Language, and had also begun (and almost completed) my Master's Degree in Hebrew language and linguistics at the Hebrew University. The time had come for some much needed rest for the weary. A trip abroad was not yet a trifling matter. Only at the end of the 1950s had Israeli tourism to Europe begun to take off, whether by airplane or aboard the ships of the Zim Company, upon whose "Theodor Herzl" I would indeed disembark in Europe.

As a matter of fact, in Israel's first decade, trips abroad were still almost exclusively taken for business purposes and were rarely a matter of popular tourism. Even in the 1960s travelers felt a certain embarrassment at choosing to go abroad, given the vigorous campaign in favor of internal tourism (on the wall of one Italian port, where the Zim boats arrived, an Israeli had scrawled in large Hebrew letters: "Israeli: Have you been to Eilat yet?")

I went to the Jerusalem offices of ISSTA, the student travel agency, and purchased round-trip boat tickets to Italy. From there I planned to travel by train around Italy and Switzerland, and finally, on to London. At the end, I would return through Paris, back to Italy, and then back to Israel. Upon my second visit to the travel agency, I happened upon an attractive young woman who was sitting quietly awaiting her turn. Our eyes met and she asked me if I spoke English. It was Terrie, my future wife. She had arrived the night before on a flight from the United States after graduating from college. She was planning, just as I was, to take a short vacation, but in Israel; after that she would begin a six-month Ulpan organized by the Jewish Agency at Kibbutz Ma'ayan Tzvi, near Zikhron Yaakov between Tel Aviv and Haifa. Terrie didn't know any Hebrew and, having arrived in Israel on her own, had difficulty communicating with the residents of the country (very few of whom spoke English in those days). We began a conversation that lasted many hours (I should say that it has lasted nearly half a century, that is, to this very day). An hour later, I invited Terrie to dinner at an oriental restaurant, and afterwards to accompany me to the Knesset plenum hall (the Knesset was then located in a temporary building on the top of Ben Yehuda Street in central Jerusalem, in the very same building as the ISSTA offices). We walked into the plenum hall, and there stood Emile Habiby on the podium, speaking in Arabic (next to him sat my friend Moshe Piamenta, later a senior professor of Arabic at the Hebrew University – and in those days, a translator from Arabic to Hebrew in the Knesset). I knew Emile quite well and had already translated one of his first stories, "Mandelbaum Gate", from Arabic, a text which was well received by the Hebrew-reading public. Habiby was an MK for the Israeli Communist Party, and would be a Knesset member for about twenty consecutive years. Terrie had trouble grasping this strange event: walking up to the Knesset hall and running into a friend, who is also a member of Parliament; hadn't I just introduced myself to her as a student at the Hebrew University? How could it be that I was close friends with a "congressman" (which is how I translated the idea of Member of Knesset to English)? (About thirty years later, Terrie and I sat side by side in the hall of the Jerusalem Theater, at the prestigious Israel Prize ceremony where Emile Habiby was one of the recipients; I was on the committee that had nominated him for the prize). Terrie was not interested in politics, and I was pleasantly surprised to see that she had no adverse reaction when I said that this member of Knesset was in the Communist Party; and furthermore that he was a Palestinian.

Terrie and I became closer in the days after our first meeting. But after a week came the time to part ways, as the date of my departure for Europe had arrived. Terrie accompanied me to Haifa and we said our goodbyes in the port next to the jetty. When I arrived in Rome I called her and suggested she join me for the trip, which was to last about a month. After a little hesitation, she accepted my proposal, and arrived by plane to the Italian capital. Together we traveled to three European countries to which neither of us had ever been.

We traveled on a budget, since we had to worry not only about food and excursions, but also sleeping and train fare between countries. Nonetheless, we returned to Israel a few weeks later without feeling that we had suffered.

Later Terrie went to Kibbutz Ma'ayan Tzvi for her Hebrew Ulpan. She likes to remind me how I would arrive at the kibbutz on Saturdays. The minibus service on the Tel Aviv Haifa line would drop me off at the bottom of the Carmel Mountain, and I would climb up to the kibbutz, which was located on the upper slope of the mountain. I would arrive huffing and puffing, and sweating (in the summer). At the end of her course, Terrie returned to Tel Aviv. We decided to get married, and the wedding took place in June 1965, almost a year after Terrie's arrival in Israel. Her Hebrew was still far from perfect, and we had to speak English together (this continued, as a habit, even after she became fluent in Hebrew). Our wedding took place at the library of the Engineers' Association House on Dizengoff Street, in the presence of good friends and close family members.

We have spent our married life in different places around the world. My work was based in Israel, where we lived in the Tel Aviv area, but my academic activities took us to many different places. At first we lived in London (where I studied linguistics on a grant from the British Council, at the University of London, or more precisely at the School of Oriental and African studies at that University). Later we moved to Oxford, where we lived for three years and where our eldest daughter, Ayelet, was born. Over the next three decades we lived for extended periods in various places in the United States and Europe: Princeton (about four years), Philadelphia (about a year), New York (about two years), and Cairo (about three years); we also returned to Oxford for a year (when I was a guest at St. Antony's College) and even spent a short period at Upsala University in Sweden. Our two other children were born during the 1970s; Avigal in Israel in 1970, and Nadav in Princeton during out stay there in 1975. Nadav's birth was a momentous event at this American university, which in the preceding decades had few Jewish students or faculty. The circumcision ceremony was held in one of the historical halls of the university; and the *mohel*, or ritual circumciser, was a properly bearded Orthodox rabbi brought in by Terrie's parents from New Brunswick, New Jersey. The event was attended by many of our friends in Princeton, as well as Terrie's parents and my mother. The university's daily newspaper published an article noting that this was the first Jewish circumcision ceremony to take place on the Princeton campus, which had begun as a theological seminary (Christian of course).

Terrie herself found her own way in Israel. She did not wish to settle for the title "professor's wife", and found an independent profession. She studied occupational therapy at Tel Aviv University and for many years worked in that profession. Later she received a Master's Degree in art therapy at Lesley College near Boston and worked in that profession simultaneously. Finally she specialized in teaching English to students with learning disabilities.

Each of our three children found her or his own way. The professions they chose are far from my field of Semitic languages and literature. Ayelet, the eldest, is a jeweler by profession. She completed her studies at the Bezalel Academy of Art and Design in Jerusalem in jewelry design and judaica, and later spent four years in Japan, where she specialized in Japanese metal techniques. She married a Canadian man from Prince Edward Island, and they have two daughters. My second daughter, Avigal, now married with two daughters, completed her studies in literature and philosophy and worked for a period at "The Marker", the online (at the time) financial supplement of *Ha'aretz*. Nadav, the youngest, completed his mandatory military service and then worked in computers, as a server manager, but at age 27 decided to go to university, and completed a degree in the departments of philosophy and arts. At the end of his studies he went on a long trip to the Indian sub-continent and East Asia. Now back in Israel, he is a computer expert.

I would like to note that the current chapter, indeed, many of the chapters of this book, were written during a semester spent in 2006 at Vanderbilt University in Nashville, Tennessee, the home of American country music. During this semester I was a member of the Department of Jewish Studies, which was being established at the time at this pleasant and vibrant university. Since I do not usually deal with Jewish studies, I decided to teach a course there on the subject of Jewish writers writing in Arabic or under the influence of Arabic culture. (My own private title for the course was "From Judah Halevi to Sami Michael".) With my students in this course I had the unusual opportunity to discuss many texts written in Hebrew or Arabic over the course of a millennium in the Middle East and in Muslim Spain. This is a subject I do not deal with as a professor in Israel, since the literature of the Jews of Muslim Spain is confined to the department of Hebrew literature, while the department of Arabic language and literature, in which I taught for thirty years, focused entirely on Arabic texts written by Arab writers. Although Israeli writers such as Sami Michael, Shimon Ballas, and Eli Amir wrote most of their works in Hebrew, some of them began their literary lives in Arabic. Once I organized a seminar in Tel Aviv on Arabic texts by Arab-Jewish writers, from Iraq and Egypt. Among those writers: Yaqub Sanua and Murad Farag (Egypt), Shalom Darwish, Anwar Shaul, and Meir Basri (Iraq), as well as Samir Naqqash, the Iraqi-Israeli who refused to give up his Iraqiness and remained an Arabic writer within a Hebrew-speaking society until the end of his days.

In these pages, I have skimmed through more than forty years of my life in Israel and abroad. The primary goal of this memoir is to reconstruct the ongoing attempts I have made to hold a discussion – even a dialogue – with Arab intellectuals and writers: Egyptians, Iraqis, Palestinians, and others, in the Middle East and elsewhere.

These efforts to create an ongoing dialogue have continued throughout my adult life, and have involved great Egyptian writers such as Mahfouz, Idris, Fawzi, and others. With them I built relations of trust and true friendship, and about each of them I will write at greater length in the chapters to follow. I have also been in a half-century's dialogue with some of the Palestinian-Arab writers in Israel, such as Emile Habiby, Jabra Nicola, Samih al-Qasim, Siham Daoud, and Michel Haddad; and also with expatriate Iraqi writers sitting in London, such as Khaled Kishtaini and Buland Al-Haydari. Despite these efforts, there have also been Egyptian and other Arab writers, whose personal and ideological formation took place during the high tide of Nasserism, who have rebuffed my attempts to talk and even to meet with me for being a citizen of the State of Israel.

CHAPTER
12

MUSTAFA

My advisor on my doctoral dissertation at Oxford University between 1965 and 1968 was Dr. Muhammad Mustafa Badawi, a native of Alexandria who was appointed lecturer in modern Arabic literature not long before my arrival in this university town. It was the first appointment in modern Arabic in the University's history. Mustafa (as he was known to his friends and students) was the person under whose supervision I sought after changing academic fields from Hebrew linguistics and language to modern Arabic literature.

Indeed my studies in Israel – at Tel Aviv University, and later at the Hebrew University in Jerusalem – had focused almost entirely on Hebrew language. When I received a British Council scholarship to study in England in 1965, I chose to focus on general linguistics at the University of London, in preparation of sorts for the dissertation I planned to write in the Hebrew language department upon my return from my year abroad.

Terrie (who was pregnant) and I settled in London and began to take advantage of all the culture this wonderful city had to offer. But several months later came an offer from Tel Aviv University (where I had previously taught Arabic, Aramaic, and other topics in the Hebrew language department). It was a very tempting offer, even if it would entail many upheavals: leaving London for Oxford, and moreover – abandoning Hebrew studies in favor of modern Arabic literature.

I had not yet studied Arabic language or literature at any university, and did not even hold a Bachelor's Degree in Arabic. All of my knowledge in the field came from my high school studies in Baghdad and from my experiences writing poetry and prose in Arabic – first in Iraq and then in Israel. I had no complaints about studying Hebrew language, nor was I eager to move into another field. But ultimately the economic factor decided in favor of the big transition: Tel Aviv University offered to cover my living and study expenses at Oxford through the completion of my doctoral studies, when I would return to Israel with the sought-after degree, I would be granted a position at the University and would help establish the department of Arabic language and literature (today known as the Department of Arabic and Islamic Studies). This offer had the potential to ensure my livelihood and academic stature, and it would spare me the need to look for an academic position, when the time came, at an institution that might not know me well. And so the decision was made: we were going to Oxford!

Now let us return to Mustafa, whose name adorns the head of this chapter. Even if Oxford had known fine European scholars of Arabic language and literature from as early as the Middle Ages, I knew that my future advisor would be the Egyptian Dr. Mustafa Badawi, as it was he who taught modern Arabic literature there. But to put my fate and future in the hands of someone from the "other side" could entail political and possibly even ideological differences. Fears of this sort filled me on my way to Oxford for my first meeting with him, but within minutes of entering his small office, a feeling of total calm came over me. His friendly bearing and warm, calm speech left no doubt that this was the kind of person I like (I should add that on the eve of the meeting I had gone to the London University Library and perused the English and Arabic works of my future mentor and was reassured that his literary approach was honest; and the scope of his expertise in Arabic and world literature was certainly impressive).

The meeting, which lasted only an hour, ended on a note of accord. Among other things Mustafa allayed any concerns I had about not having studied literature, not to mention Arabic literature, in any university setting. As to the subject of the doctorate, we agreed to seriously consider the possibility that I would write a dissertation on the Egyptian writer Naguib Mahfouz, whose fiftieth birthday had recently been celebrated in Egypt. I was familiar with Mahfouz's work to some extent and now I set about reading those of his works that I was not familiar with and reviewing the critical literature on his oeuvre. From that same meeting I stopped being a potential Hebrew scholar and returned to my roots in Arabic language and literature.

Within a few weeks of our arrival in Oxford, our first daughter, Ayelet, was born. She spent her first years in Oxford (to be precise, in Eynsham, a village adjacent to the university town, from where I would go each day to the libraries and institutes at Oxford). Mustafa gave me virtually absolute freedom in seeking a direction and starting point for my dissertation. In the first months I read one after another of Mahfouz's works (which at the time numbered about twenty novels and five collections of short stories), and began by writing critical summaries of each work. Mustafa would read what I wrote and make comments here and there. He was a wonderfully liberal adviser and gave me the freedom to do as I pleased; what mattered to him was that the writing be "logical" and that I look at the works as literary texts and not as social, political, or philosophical "testimonies". Although my orientation toward the study of language was some- what foreign to Mustafa, he quickly understood my obsessive desire to deal with the writer's language and the language of fictive dialogue – and he began to encourage me to continue examining the works in this spirit.

Within six months of beginning to work with Mustafa, I began to consolidate the general direction of the dissertation; it would be a systematic examination of the development of Mahfouz's narrative writing in terms of the treatment of time, characters, speech, etc., and an attempt to identify the works' influences. One of the central chap- ters in my dissertation dealt with Mahfouz's *Cairo Trilogy*. This work, which spanned some 1500 pages in the Arabic original, recounts the story of Egyptian society between the two World Wars. At its center is a family from the merchant class and its transition over a quarter century from patriarchalism to a degree of modernity, in terms of education, women's status, political tendencies, etc. In this chapter I focused on a number of topics, two of which I will expand upon briefly here. The first topic: the influences. Egyptian critics had tended to treat the work as belonging to the family trilogy genre and being influenced primarily by the famous family trilogies in Western literature (Galsworthy, Balzac, etc.). My analysis uncovered a different and unexpected aspect, namely, the influence of the novel *Buddenbrooks* by the great German writer Thomas Mann (1875– 1955). I came to this conclusion through a comparative analysis of the structure of the plot through the changes that permeate the inner consciousness of the protagonists in the wake of social and political changes. Eventually, after my dissertation was published as a book in the Netherlands, I came upon an exciting piece of evidence that indirectly confirmed my thesis: in a letter written by Mahfouz to a friend who was living in Europe in the late 1930s, I discovered that the author was aware of Mann's novel and even asked the friend in Europe to buy and send him a copy of the English translation that had just been published. This dispelled my detractors' claims that Mann was not among the European authors known in the Arab world in the 1930s and 1940s, and that it was implausible for *Buddenbrooks* to have had any influence on Arabic literature. The other reason for which I mention this chapter on Mahfouz's trilogy: I measured the amount of time covered in the plot against the amount of descriptive text in each one of the volumes, and I found that the author achieves a clear process of reduction over the course of the scenes and chapters in the book (for example the first, "patriarchal", volume, which covers a year and a half, spans 580 pages, while the third, "modern", volume describes nine years in 395 pages); the same goes for the length and structure of the sentences and the extent of external and psychological descriptions. Accordingly, this chapter of the dissertation is entitled "The Changing Rhythm", the eventual title of my monograph about Mahfouz, published in English in Leiden, the Netherlands in 1973.

I will not write any more about my dissertation at Oxford, since I am more concerned with describing my life and that of my family in this wonderful setting and in the company of Mustafa and of other friends, Israelis and others.

Since I have known Oxford, there have always been a good number of Israelis studying there. Every time over the past forty years that I have counted the number of Israeli students (more or less) at Oxford, I have discovered that at any given time there were twenty to thirty doctoral students, each spending three to four years there. One of the students from Israel at Oxford along with me (at least for part of my time there) was my childhood friend from Baghdad, David Semah. He arrived at Oxford a year after I did and returned to Israel about a year after me. David had written Arabic poetry even as a young man and taught me, around 1949, before either of us left for Israel, the basics of Arabic prosody, enabling me to write (and publish) poems in classic Arabic meters instead of the prose poems I had written until then.

Our friendship had grown during our first years in Israel as we joined left-wing circles together and established the Tel Aviv Arabic Literary Circle. After completing his Master's Degree at the Hebrew University with honors, Haifa University proposed to David to get his PhD abroad in Arabic literature; upon his return he would join the faculty of the department they were planning to establish there. His heart tended toward medieval Arabic literature, but the University preferred modern Arabic literature. Thus David also reached Dr. Mustafa Badawi, under whose supervision he wrote a dissertation about four literary critics who wrote primarily in the first half of the twentieth century in Egypt (this book had a great impact upon its publication by Brill in The Netherlands).

And so it came to pass that, beginning in 1966, Mustafa Badawi had two Israeli doctoral students, his only doctoral students at the time. We were never given the slightest feeling of foreignness or alienation for belonging to an enemy nation. I remember that in May 1967, as the atmosphere of war between Israel and its neighbors intensified, we continued to work with Mustafa in perfect harmony. At the end of May, Mustafa invited the two of us with our families (David with his wife and children and Terrie and I with our daughter, Ayelet) for Sunday lunch. It was a sun-drenched day, and we all had a wonderful time on the Badawi's lawn, in spite of the worries that loomed in all of our hearts at the political situation. In the midst of the party, Mustafa drew David and me aside and told us that we should not worry about the imminent events. If a war should break out and the transfer of our living stipends from Israel be disrupted, he would do all he could to ensure that our families would not suffer, searching, if necessary, for alternate financial sources. This conversation did not include any discussion about the brewing situation in the Middle East following Nasser's demand to expel the UN forces from the Straits of Tiran. Both David and I were grateful to our advisor for his devotion to his students. We all feared that a war between Egypt and Israel would be long and its damages great.

And then the Six Day War broke out in June 1967, and after just a few days the armies of Egypt, Syria, and Jordan were defeated. We breathed a sigh of relief, of course, even if our worries were renewed within days as calls came from within Israel to summarily annex parts of the conquered territories. In my long conversations with David at the time, we had a sense, if only vaguely, that the disdain for our Arab neighbors that was spreading among the Israeli public and the aspiration to annex more and more land, would ultimately lead to an all-out altercation with the peoples of the region, and that the ultimate end of this military victory would be an unprecedented political disaster.

Only several months later did I discuss the "situation" with Mustafa. He was clearly shocked by the outcome of the war. As an Egyptian patriot, he was furious that Israel had conquered Egyptian territory, but I never heard him speak of Israel as "a military fortress" or as heading an "imperialistic plot", and he always distinguished between the different worldviews within the Israeli public and even among its leadership. Throughout the years of the "War of Attrition", during which I visited Oxford on occasion from my home in Tel Aviv, we held quiet political conversations, never with raised voices. There was no substantive disagreement between us, but each of us saw parts of the reality that the other could not.

With the arrival of peace with Egypt following Sadat's visit to Israel, Mustafa supported the Camp David Accords, and as far as I know this got him into difficult arguments with some of his Arab and English colleagues, who saw the peace as an American-imposed deal that did not restore all of Egypt's lost honor. My academic cooperation with Mustafa continued even upon my return to Israel from my studies in England. In 1970, he and a group of professors of Arabic literature at British universities founded an annual journal (which later became a quarterly) called the *Journal of Arabic Literature*. For years this was the only academic journal outside the Arab world supporting the study of Arabic literature, medieval and modern. I was invited to take part in the endeavor even before the publication of the first issues of the journal, and an article I wrote, analyzing Naguib Mahfouz's short story, "Zaabalawi", appeared in the first issue. In the ten years following, I contributed no less than six studies to the journal, dealing with Egyptian, Lebanese, and Iraqi writers.

We had another cooperative endeavor in the 80s, when Mustafa was asked to edit a volume in the series "History of Arabic Literature". Badawi's volume dealt with contemporary Arabic literature, published by Cambridge University Press in 1992. Each chapter of the book was written by a different scholar, each according to his field of expertise. I was asked to write the chapter dealing with neo-classical Arabic poetry, those works by Arabic poets from the mid-nineteenth century until the 1950s. This poetry is notable for its aspiration to emulate the traditional poetic form, a sort of continuation of Arabic poetry of the Muslim Golden Age, while its contents were meant to be "modern". This school gave rise to some of the great twentieth-century poets, among them the Egyptian Ahmad Shawqi and the Iraqi Al-Juwahiri. Badawi was aware of my personal opinion that it is possible to write "new content" using old tools, and I had already published an article demonstrating that an early twentieth-century translation of the English poet Shelley to classical Arabic, lost the fundamental meaning of the English original, virtually transforming the text into a love poem of the kind found in droves in the annals of Arabic literature. But nonetheless, it was this chapter of all chapters that I was asked to write. Since the subject was new for me, I took several months to read most of the *diwan*s (poetic opuses) of the neo-classical poets (I must have gone through 300-400 such *diwan*s), and the chapter I wrote (about fifty pages long) appeared at the beginning of Mustafa's volume. Later the entire book was translated to Arabic and published in Saudi Arabia. I was pleased, upon receipt of a copy of the Arabic translation, to find that my chapter had been translated faithfully and with great precision (taking up about 100 pages of the thick Saudi volume).

In 1993, when Mustafa retired from active teaching, an academic conference was held in his honor at St. John's College, Oxford, with the participation of his close friends and colleagues, including his former students. David Semah and I were among the lecturers at the conference. In my lecture I presented findings from research I was conducting at the time on the Arabic translations of the Old and New Testaments and discussed at length the influence on Arabic literature and on modern literary Arabic of the translations done in Beirut in the mid-nineteenth century by American and French missionaries. My lecture provoked a long discussion and Mustafa himself expressed his satisfaction that I had "smuggled" the Bible into the conference we had held in his honor.

In the 1990s Mustafa was diagnosed with an illness that kept him from moving freely outside of his house. Therefore Terrie and I made sure to visit his home in Wheatley, near Oxford, every time we passed through England to see him and his warm and friendly Dutch wife, Micke. These visits were among the great joys we knew. Located on an ancient Roman road, the Badawi's house was apparently built in the seventeenth century, and its walls were made of hewn stone. At the risk of sounding too "romantic", I will say that the scenery of the ancient village, with its historical churches, filled the visitor from Israel with a tantalizing world of experiences; but the true experience was in spending time with friends with whom our courageous friendship lasted for more than forty years, despite the often troubling situation in the Middle East. My memories from the British village of the Egyptian Badawi are one of the precious gifts I have received in my life.

13

TRANSLATING LITERATURE

I have spent many hours, days, and nights over the course of my life translating poetry from Arabic to Hebrew. Today my drawers and files contain a variety of short and long poems translated and published by me over more than fifty years. In my estimation, the number of these translations lies somewhere between 1,000 and 1,500, most published in the Israeli press, periodicals of all sorts and literary supplements of the daily newspapers. I am not ashamed to admit that my fascination with translating poetry borders on obsession, but unlike other obsessions, to translate a poem, for me, is to find a moment of calm, much like for a player of chess or bridge. When I am weary from my daily toils, I pick up a book of poetry and choose something to translate; and if the result is to my liking, a feeling of satisfaction permeates my body.

I had come to Israel from Iraq with three books that required a special export authorization from the Iraqi Ministry of Education and Culture. Among these were two slim anthologies of poetry by young Iraqi poets, some of whom I knew from Baghdad's "literary" cafés. The third book was a fascinating critical work by an Egyptian author, about trends in Arabic poetry in the twentieth century. The author included the partial or complete text of many poems in the book, and it was thanks to this that I became acquainted with these poems.

As I have already noted, I arrived in Israel with no knowledge of Hebrew but with a dream in my heart: to master the Hebrew language and to translate a selection of these poems, whose conception in the poets' minds and notebooks I had sometimes witnessed in Baghdad. No sooner had I conquered the Hebrew language than I began to translate, driven by my personal association with these young poets. Rarely did I try my hand at translation in the opposite direction; only on the rare occasion that I was beseeched to translate a Hebrew poem to Arabic did I try my hand at that. One of the poets who asked – and whose request I could not refuse – was Yehuda Amichai, who, in my mind and in the minds of many others, represents Israeli poetry at its very best. The text I translated was a rather long poem that Amichai had been commissioned to write in honor of the construction of a decorative gate at the entrance to Jerusalem in the 1980s. The intention was to etch the poem on the gate alongside its Arabic translation. The project was never realized, and I do not know what Amichai did with the poem he had written for the occasion. My translation, which I had labored over quite a bit, no longer had any use, and after the poet's death I sent the translation to his widow, Hannah, for her to include in her late husband's archive.

I recall another poem or two that I translated to Arabic: when Alexander Penn's collected poems, *Along the Way*, was published in 1956, I translated a few of the shorter poems at the request of Emile Habiby, and they appeared in an article I wrote about the collection for the Haifa-based literary monthly, *Al-Jadid*. And, last but not least: the well-known poem by H.N. Bialik, "I didn't win light in a windfall", which I translated into Arabic, preserving both meter and rhyme, for publication in *Al-Fajar*, Rashid Hussein's monthly. Later on, Rashid Hussein would translate – in meter, but not in strict rhyme – a selection of Bialik's poetry that was published in a remarkable edition by the Hebrew University in 1966.

Let us return to the Hebrew translations. The first of my translations to be published was a poem by the Haifaian poet, Issam Abassi, who was associated with the Communist Party. The poem was called "My Village" and its translation appeared in 1954 in the periodical *Ner* (Candle), the mouthpiece of the now defunct "Brit Shalom" (Peace Alliance), edited by R. Benjamin and later by Dr. Sharshevsky. The translation was crude and prosaic, and thus lost the sing-song nature that gave classical Arabic poetry its poetic quality. I had not yet found the key to unlock the connection between the classical Arabic meters used by the Arab poets until the mid-twentieth century and beyond, and the European meter used in contemporary Hebrew poetry.

About a year later, I came to the conclusion that in order to translate Arabic poetry to Hebrew it was necessary to use the "European" meters (such as Iambic and trochaic), without which there would be no compensation for the loss of the Arabic meter. Moreover, it is impossible to translate the monorhymed Arabic poems with a singular rhyme in Hebrew, but rather an alternating rhyme pattern must be used. The first poems I translated according to these principles were those I published in *Kol Ha'Am* in the mid-50s, which was edited at the time by Alexander Penn, as I wrote in an earlier chapter; I would publish my translations in Maki's newspaper for about a decade. Thematically, these poems were replete with the spirit of struggle and hope for the future, including poems condemning war and supporting the idea of peace. Poems with individualistic content, not to mention experimental or modern poems written in the spirit of contemporary international poetry (which existed in Arabic starting in the 40s), were considered by us "progressives", as we called ourselves, to be a product of decadent culture that ostensibly sanctified form over content.

In 1964, a section of a special issue of the literary quarterly *Keshet*, edited by Aharon Amir, was dedicated to translations from contemporary Arabic literature and articles on the subject. A large part of these translations were my own, and I also published an article there about the development of the poetic forms in contemporary Arabic literature ("New Forms Seeking Content"). The issue sparked great interest in Israel, but not long after its appearance I traveled to England to complete my studies, and for about three years lost touch with the world of translation and poetry. Upon my return to Israel at the end of 1968, Amir and I began to plan a special issue of *Keshet* that would be entirely dedicated to Arabic literature, with a special focus on developments in the region after the 1967 war. The special issue (Issue 47) appeared in 1970, and it included an abundance of poetic translations – most, if not all, of my handiwork. Aside from the poems, the issue included several articles, most of which were written by academic writers, on subjects in Arabic literature that I had singled out in advance. Nissim Rejwan wrote a long essay on the motif of rage that appeared after 1967, and Shimon Ballas reviewed a number of literary works published in the Arab world since 1967 (and shortly beforehand). Ballas would later use this paper as the basis for his doctoral thesis at the Sorbonne, whose Hebrew translation would appear as a dense book entitled *Arabic Literature in the Shadow of War* in Am Oved's "Horizons" series in 1978. In addition, the issue included two academic papers by lecturers of Arabic literature at the

Hebrew University, Milson and Moreh, along with an article of mine on the works of Fadwa Tuqan, the poetess from Nablus.

As for the poems themselves, this was the first time modernist poems were chosen for their poetic quality and for their modernism per se. Poems by Adonis, the exiled Syrian poet, and by members of the Beirut quarterly, *Shi'r* (Poetry), were the heroes of the day. Most of the reviews of *Keshet* 47 dwelled upon these poems, which was a surprise for many of us at the journal. The immediate result: one of the editors at Sifriyat Po'alim (The Workman's Library), rang me and offered me to edit an anthology of modern Arabic poetry for his publishing house. Without batting an eye, I said yes; I even decided, in that same telephone conversation, upon the name of the collection: "The Pharpar River: Young Syrian and Lebanese poetry" (Pharpar is the biblical name of one of the big rivers of Damascus). The collection included selections from the poetry of five poets, of the crème de la crème of Arabic modernism in our day: Adonis, Unsi Al-Hajj, Shawqi Abi-Shaqra, Fuad Rifaqa, and Muhamad Al-Maghout. The elegant book reached many private and public bookshelves, but it did not, in my opinion, have a proper public impact; the October 1973 war broke out just a few weeks after the book's release and struck an unexpected blow that resonated throughout Israel. Another two collections: a collection of the Nazarene poet Michel Haddad ("Hitztabrut", meaning "accumulation") was published by The United Kibbutz Publishers in 1979. The collection included poems that I translated and also poems translated by Eliyahu Agassi, Menahem Milson, Hannah Amit-Kochavi, and Naim Araidi; and a collection of the poems of the Haifa poetess Siham Daud entitled *I Love in White Ink*, translated by me and published by Sifriyat Po'alim (1973).

At this point I would like to dedicate a few words to Aharon Amir (1923–2008), the editor of *Keshet* (and later, *The New Keshet*). My friendship with Aharon was for me a godsend. Aharon and I were not of one mind regarding the fateful issues facing Israel, above all the question of our relations with our Arab neighbors. Aharon never abandoned his views, which were fundamentally Canaanite (footnote overleaf),[4] but as the editor of the most important literary–cultural quarterly of the 1960s, 70s, and 80s, his cultural-political bent never steered *Keshet* to the right. Amir worked hard to keep his journal, in its original (as well as its "New" version), as open and as removed as possible from any nationalist-propagandist orientation, as was the case with the late Dr. Israel Eldad-Scheib's *Sulam* (Ladder), published in those same years, and *Ha'uma* (The Nation), which appears to this day. *Keshet*'s pages included young writers with clearly "dovish" temperaments such as Amos Oz and A.B. Yehoshua, as well as two interesting writers of Middle-Eastern-Jewish origin who wrote in English. The first was the brilliant Cairo-born essayist, Jacqueline Shohet-Kahanoff, who, until Amir "discovered" her, had no connection with the world of Israeli literature. The articles she wrote from her home in Israel appeared mostly in Jewish and Zionist publications in Israel and the USA. Amir translated and published a series of essays by Jacqueline in *Keshet* entitled "The Levantine Generation", in which she put forth, in a style that has captivated the hearts of her readers ever since,[5] experiences from her childhood and youth in Egypt in the company of her girlfriends – a charming cosmopolitan bunch. This generation of young people, who had no sense of religious or ethnic contradictions or discrimination, is presented in "The Levantine Generation" as the embodiment of multiculturalism, an experience made fundamentally possible, in Jacqueline's view, by "Levantinism" – the mingling of east and west in a relaxed and tolerant environment. Jacqueline suggested that if Israel would be more "Levantine", it would be able to live with its neighbors according to the model she presented. These articles influenced in different ways the thinking and worldviews of many of the 1970s generation and onwards, and in any event replaced the stigma attached to the word "Levantine" with more positive connotations. Thanks to Amir, even though she could not write in Hebrew, Jacqueline herself became a well-known Israeli writer and her articles were published later on in many newspapers and journals in Israel.

The second of these essayists was Nissim Rejwan, a Baghdad Jew

4 The Canaanite Movement, founded in 1939, was a cultural-artistic-philosophical movement associated with the political Right. Its members saw ancient Hebrew culture and the geographical association with the land of Israel, rather than religious affiliation, as the defining element of secular Hebrew or Israeli culture.

5 An anthology of Kahanoff's works, titled *Mongrels and Marvels: The Levantine Writings of Jacqueline Shohet-Kahanoff*, was published by the Stanford University Press in 2011,edited by Deborah Starr and Sasson Somekh.

who came to Israel with the mass immigration wave of 1950, having already gained experience writing in the Baghdad daily *Iraq Times*. Rejwan, who was skilled in writing in English, worked for a period at the English-language daily *Jerusalem Post*. In *Keshet*, many of his essays about Arabic culture, past and present, were published (including in Issue 47). Rejwan's non-academic style was geared towards the general educated public, and his direct and rich prose gave his essays an intellectual character that reflected his respect for Arabic culture throughout its history. Many of Rejwan's essays were published in the original English by the University of Florida Press, and his three-volume autobiography was published beginning in the nineties by Texas University Press. It should be noted that, while his historical–political articles appeared on various occasions in Hebrew, his impressive autobiography was never published in Israel. A propos Jacqueline Kahanoff: it was Nissim Rejwan who introduced her to Aharon Amir. Amir introduced us in turn, and we quickly forged a warm friendship that lasted up until Kahanoff's death in 1979.

My relationship with Amir continued for four decades, during which time I got to know him up close as a man of culture and as a marvelous editor. For more than ten years we lived in the same apartment building in Ramat Aviv, and I would regularly bring him short reviews I had written, to be published in the final section of each issue of *Keshet*. The advantage of these reviews was that the reviewers were not required to sign their names, but rather used initials (sometimes fictitious ones), and were thus freed from the need to praise or disparage according to the protocols of the personal relationship between the critic and his subject (not to mention that, in such a small country as Israel, everyone is acquainted).

I greatly admire Amir's literary judgment and editing style. I should start by saying that, despite our ideological differences, he entrusted me entirely with the form and content of Issue 47 of *Keshet* (and even credited me in the title page of the issue as its editor), reducing his own editorial role to "technical" tasks such as transliterations and stylistic consistency. Many of the poetic translations he did not touch at all, and for that I am grateful to him to this day, forty years later.

But the principle of editorial non-interference was not always to be taken for granted with Amir. In 1964, I had submitted an article to him for Issue 24, and when he returned the proofs to me, I was shocked to find that the article had been edited and corrected through and through. Among other things, Amir replaced the Aramaic or Aramaic-inflected phrases, which I was so fond of, with "pure" Hebrew expressions. In those days I was working at the secretariat of the Academy for Hebrew Language, and did not consider my Hebrew to warrant any editing. I was very angry, and even considered asking him to return the article without publishing it, but then I reconsidered. Many years later those proofs surfaced, and I found that my youthful arrogance had been baseless, and that most of Amir's corrections were reasonable and even beneficial.

And last but not least: When I first sent a poem of mine and the translation of a short story from Arabic to *Keshet* in 1960, I did not mention that I wrote regularly for *Kol HaAm* (as I mentioned, most of the things I wrote in *Kol Ha'am* were under pseudonyms). A short while later, Amir published both pieces in Issue 6 of *Keshet*. I thought I had pulled one over on him, but later it turned out that he already knew of my "shady past", but this did not deter him from publishing my pieces. Thanks to Aharon Amir I came out of my hiding place in *Kol Ha'am* into the open and dynamic world of *Keshet*, the most important journal of those days.

CHAPTER
14

HAIM BLANC

Of all the scholars with whom I studied, in Israel and abroad, none did I idolize as much as Haim Blanc. Although I am grateful to and fond of many of my teachers (among them truly great scholars), to this day it is Haim, who died an untimely death, whom I feel luckiest to have met and for my years of friendship with such a true genius.

In 1961 I went to study at the Hebrew University in Jerusalem, after completing my undergraduate studies at Tel Aviv University, to specialize in Hebrew language. Blanc taught in Jerusalem at the time in the general linguistics department and had already, at the age of thirty-five, earned an international reputation as a scholar of Arabic dialects. I voluntarily chose to enroll in two of his courses that same year, and during the two years I spent at the Hebrew University, I did not miss a single one of his classes, even though they were not part of my requirements.

Blanc grew up in the United States, and one could detect the American accent behind his rich Hebrew (and Arabic) speech. Born in Romania, he and his family moved to Paris when he was very young, and when he was a boy they moved to the United States, where he spent the formative years of his education and out of which he emerged feeling American through and through. Still, several languages were deeply embedded in him: Yiddish, Hebrew, French, and English, and perhaps also Russian.

From the moment I met him I was drawn above all to his unique personality, which exuded friendship and warmth, and also to the abundant curiosity apparent in almost every sentence that rolled off his tongue, as the saying by Terentius goes: "Homo sum: humani nil a me alienum puto" (I am a human being, so nothing human is strange to me). However, Haim could be blunt and impatient at times, when he heard people speaking "nonsense" about linguistic matters; and didn't so many of us like to wax philosophical on questions of language and to conjecture, often tenuously, about etymologies? This kind of thing really got on his nerves, and Haim would scoff at his interlocutors with uncharacteristic sharpness.

And I haven't yet mentioned that Haim Blanc was blind – not from birth, but following a war-time accident. This is how it happened: as a young officer in the American army, Haim was sent to Europe as a liaison officer with the French headquarters in occupied Austria, because of his knowledge of languages. At the end of the War, he returned to the United States to continue his studies at Harvard University, which had been deferred during World War II. With the outbreak of the war in Israel in 1948, the young linguist volunteered for the Foreign Volunteers Unit and came to Israel to participate in the war that would determine the fate of the land. Upon his arrival in Israel he was sent to fight with the Harel Division on the road to Jerusalem, and there he was injured and blinded in battle. Haim was sent to the United States for treatment and for training for life as a blind person, and when he returned to Israel he was determined to put down roots. He enrolled at the Hebrew University and began to specialize in the spoken Arabic language, under the guidance of such prominent Jerusalemite scholars as Goitein and Polotzky (I should note that Haim completed his B.A. at Harvard under the guidance of one of the great linguists of our generation, Roman Jakobson, writing his thesis on the influences of the Slavic languages on Yiddish). Blanc finished his doctorate in Jerusalem in less than three years, focusing on the Druze dialect in the north of Israel. This study was published in Jerusalem in 1953, in English, as "Studies in North Palestinian Arabic". A year later, Haim married a young American woman, Judy, and from then on the couple lived in Jerusalem, where they had a daughter and two sons. In this period, around 1955, I happened to meet him and even to visit his apartment along with a common friend. This short visit remained with me as a wonderful experience, which I later associated with the man for many years.

In 1958, Haim returned to Harvard with a grant from that institution. There, he researched the linguistic environment in Baghdad. As a result of this sabbatical he published (at Harvard University) the best-known of his works – *Communal Dialects in Baghdad* – in which he solved a series of conundrums regarding the dialects of the Iraqi capital.

Blanc was a professor at the Hebrew University from the 1950s up until the early 1980s when he was diagnosed with a degenerative disease, from which he eventually died. He continued his academic pursuits of linguistic questions pertaining to Arabic and general linguistics. In the last decade of his scholarship he became particularly interested in the Egyptian dialects. He dealt, with a large degree of success, with a series of complex historical questions that had been given no scientific answer until then. It should be said that linguist "fieldwork" (and that word does certainly describe the study of dialects) necessitates intimate contact with the site and with speakers of the language, who serve as informants. For Blanc, the mission was possible (even if not at all simple) in the case of the Druze community in Israel; but research of the languages of Iraq and Egypt posed a series of requirements that Blanc could not fulfill. In the case of Baghdad it required not only staying in the Iraqi capital, something that was (and still is) not at all possible for an Israeli scholar, but also listening to "witnesses" and precisely transliterating what they say. Moreover, Baghdad had three different dialects spoken by three different religions: Muslims, Jews, and Christians. Most of his linguistic informants from the Muslim and Christian communities he met in the United States while at Harvard, while the Jewish informants he met in Israel. Despite all these difficulties, Blanc produced a masterful study, which upset some of the commonly held opinions in the study of dialects.

In the years in which I took Blanc's classes, I would meet him on the old campus of the Hebrew University at Givat Ram, and later also around his home in Talbiye, where he would walk with his seeing-eye dog (named "Abu el-'Izz", as I recall). If you would hold out a hand to help him walk in the right direction, he would adamantly shake loose from your grip, as if in defense of the wonderful dog's professional honor. In class, when writing down examples in chalk on the board, he would not allow his students to approach the board and make corrections when he had written one word on top of another. The sense of independence and the pride in overcoming the disability was deeply rooted in his consciousness.

When I returned from my studies in England in 1969, we renewed our friendship, even more closely. I would go up to Jerusalem from time to time in order to visit him and his wife at their home; once or twice he went to the trouble of coming to Tel Aviv to visit me at my home in Ramat Aviv (one time he came on his own to a ceremony at Tel Aviv University where I was being granted a chair in Arabic literature; my insistence that the event was not important enough for him to bother to come to Tel Aviv was in vain). Haim thrilled me when he invited me to lecture in a course he was giving on the Egyptian dialects, after I completed my dissertation at Oxford about the works of Naguib Mahfouz. I tried to focus on the "Egyptian" influences in the writer's style, but at the end of my lecture Haim continued to speak to me, not about the linguistic aspects (which were a subject of secondary importance in the dissertation), but about the works themselves and about Mahfouz's narrative art, which were the main focus of my research. I was surprised to discover how abreast he was of developments in contemporary Arabic literature. Indeed, he employed excellent and trustworthy readers and talented assistants to read to him. Indeed, the extent of his reading and up-to-date knowledge was amazing. He was read to regularly in three "European" languages (English, French, and Russian) and in two Semitic languages (Hebrew and Arabic), sometimes even outdoing many of his seeing colleagues. I remember a case in which I gave him a copy of an article I had published in an academic journal abroad. That same day, just before midnight, Haim called me to critique something I had written in a footnote at the bottom of one of the pages. I asked him how he had managed to read the article so quickly, but with his characteristic quiet self-confidence he asked me a question that was more important than the one I had asked.

Two or three years before his death his health took a turn for the worse (he suffered from multiple sclerosis), and he had to retire from active teaching at the university; but he did not abandon his research in Arabic dialects, and some of his most important articles appeared in his final years. I recall with what joy he gave me a copy of an article he had written about the history of the Cairene dialect, which had been published in Beirut, in fact, as part of a volume published by the Saint Joseph University in Beirut in honor of the linguist Henri Fleisch. The article was apparently published in 1973, but copies of it reached Jerusalem only seven or eight years later.

About a year before his death a traumatic event happened as a result of which Blanc lost what remained of his independence. His

dog died suddenly after eating poison dispensed by the municipality
to kill rodents, and Haim was left housebound and unable to walk
around freely in his beloved city of Jerusalem. Because of his weakened state, he could not travel to the United States to practice with
a new dog. In his last months he was bed-ridden and almost unable
to lift his head from his pillow. In this difficult period I was blessed
with a large portion of my teacher Haim Blanc's time: we spoke on
the phone almost every day – long, ongoing conversations that sometimes lasted into the wee hours of the night. In these conversations
he also spoke about himself and about the years in which he had been
young and with acute vision. Just days before his death, I returned
from a tour of several universities in the United States. I went to visit
him and told him about the places I had visited and about the
common friends I had seen. All of a sudden, Haim made a great effort
and lifted his head from his pillow and said to me: "In another three
months, when my condition improves, I will be able to visit those
places and meet the friends whom you met." A tear rolled from my
eyes upon hearing these words, which I knew would never come to
be, and I was glad that Haim could not see this. Three or four days
later I opened the morning paper and saw the death notice of
Professor Haim Blanc.

Let us return to Blanc's book on the communal dialects of Baghdad.
In this book Blanc set out to research a linguistic phenomenon that
does not exist in many places, if at all, outside of Baghdad: three religious communities (Muslim, Christian, and Jewish), each with its
own dialect. When different languages exist side by side in the same
area, it is usually evidence of one linguistic groups' recent arrival at
a place where there is an established lingual community (usually the
majority community). One assumes this to be a temporary situation,
and that the new immigrant community will settle in, adopt the
language of the established majority, and that only vestiges will
remain of its original language. The situation in Baghdad is clearly
different. Each of the city's three communities has lived there for a
long time, but there is no evidence of merging between the dialects
of the different communities. And furthermore: while the Jewish
dialect and the Christian dialect do have similarities (Blanc called

these two dialects "qeltu" types), they are completely different from the dialect of the Muslim majority. From his in-depth research among the speakers of the different dialects and also from quotations and linguistic sequences recorded by travelers and writers one or two hundred years earlier, Blanc derived the following facts:

The dialect of the Jews of Baghdad is in fact the original dialect used by most residents of Baghdad, regardless of religion (of course, in the languages used by the Jews themselves we find certain elements taken from Hebrew and Aramaic). Over the course of the last two hundred years, waves upon waves of speakers of the Bedouin dialect (a dialect of the "gelet" type) came from the south, and for years the language of the immigrants spread and became the language of the majority.

But why didn't the language of the Jews and the Christians also change? The answer is simple: since the Bedouins who settled in and around Baghdad were Muslims, their linguistic sphere of influence did not reach the minority communities, who lived, for the most part, in their own areas and never intermarried with the Muslim newcomers. And thus Blanc solved the riddle that had always puzzled scholars of dialects, and provided a scholarly "model" that combined the geographical with the chronological dimension in the study of language.

Blanc did amazing things in the study of Arabic language, among other things studying pan-Arabic dialectical phenomena that had not been previously studied (for example, the "pseudo-dual"[6] that exists in various Arabic dialects), and also the grammatical theory of medieval classical Arabic and its connection to contemporary dialects. And he did not shy away from questions of Hebrew language either: not long after settling in Jerusalem he was invited by his friend, the Hebrew poet T. Carmi (also born in the United States), a founding editor at the literary weekly, *Massa*, to write a column on language. Blanc accepted the invitation and for nearly three years (between 1952 and 1954) he published a language column under the name H. Kablan (Blanc with the letters scrambled). His pieces aroused a storm of protest from those Israeli linguists who taught Hebrew language and grammar. Blanc's free and genuinely linguistic

6 "Pseudo-dual" refers to a form in the spoken language of Cairo in which "a pair of" things can mean "a few" or even "plenty of".

opinions shocked and angered them, since Blanc expressed the opinion that linguistic "mistakes" that occur in the speech of native speakers of a language are not necessarily mistakes, and it is very likely that over the course of time they will become accepted and even "correct" (after all, doesn't every language have foundations that were at first considered mistakes?). These opinions were already accepted in linguistic circles around the world, but in Israel the method of "don't say A, say B" still reigned, even in the linguistic columns published in the Israeli press in the mid-twentieth century.

Blanc was never elected a member of the Academy of Hebrew Language, not even when his linguistic achievements brought great honor to Israel, and not when his views on Israeli Hebrew, which were innovative and unusual in the 1950s, became a matter of consensus. Perhaps the reason he was not chosen is that his professional field does not fall, academically speaking, under the category of "Hebrew studies" but in that of general linguistics, even though some of his most remarkable works dealt with Jewish dialects.

15

SATURDAY EVENINGS
AT THE GOITEINS

It was not until 1974 that I met Professor Shlomo Dov Goitein, one of the great modern scholars of Islam and the pioneer scholar of Cairo Geniza research. This was due to the fact that my early studies in Israel had focused on Hebrew and not on Arabic or Islam; and that only upon my arrival at Oxford in 1965 had I made the transition to Arabic studies. Nonetheless, Goitein's name was more than familiar to me from remarks I had heard from friends and fellow Iraqis who had arrived in Israel, like myself, at the beginning of the 1950s. They talked about the stern "jekke" (a mildly derogatory nickname for a German Jew), who tried to dissuade them from studying in the Arabic department and advised them first to integrate into the country and serve in the army before going to study at the university. Thus, from a distance, I had received a less than positive impression of the man. Around 1965, however, I read and was very impressed by his work on Arab–Jewish relations, written for a general readership: *Jews and Arabs: Their Contacts through the Ages*. How could a person with such respect for the past and traditions of our Arab neighbors have behaved as my friends had described him? Perhaps they had misrepresented him.

The first time I met Goitein in person was in 1974, on the Tel Aviv University campus, on the occasion of an international conference on Jews in Muslim lands. The conference centered around the Cairo Geniza and its documents – Goitein's life's work. In our fleeting, almost chance, conversation, in one of the campus corridors, Goitein told me that he had seen the anthology *The World of Naguib Mahfouz*, which I had published two years earlier, incorporating a

selection of Mahfouz's texts in the original Arabic. I was surprised
that he, a medievalist, was so familiar with modern Arabic literature
and scholarship. He added that he would like to see a similar
anthology published, with reproductions of Arabic language Geniza
documents (as opposed to the majority of the documents, which were
in Hebrew or Judeo-Arabic). Finally, he asked me if I was considering
taking a sabbatical, and suggested that I consider Princeton
University. As it happened, I had just been thinking of planning a
sabbatical for myself and my family, after six years of teaching at Tel
Aviv. A short while after sending my request to Princeton, I received
a positive, though oddly formulated, response: although they were
not in need of a guest lecturer in Arabic literature, and despite budg-
etary constraints, they had decided to invite me. So they wrote. I was
overjoyed, and I wrote to Goitein thanking him for his advice. Not
only was Princeton a leading university (not only in physics but also
in Arabic and Islamic studies), but it was also located a short distance
from my wife's parents in New Jersey. Goitein himself lived in
Princeton, but was not associated with the University or its
Department of Near Eastern Studies. Rather, he was a member of the
Institute for Advanced Study, an independent and highly respected
institution (where none other than Albert Einstein had been a fellow
in his years in the United States).

In August 1974, my family and I arrived in beautiful Princeton,
where we were placed in an apartment in the visiting professors'
housing. The next morning I woke up and, with Goitein's telephone
number in hand, I prepared to call him and tell him we had arrived.
I hesitated a moment because of the hour, and decided to wait until
9 a.m., so as not to awaken the elderly man. I rang, and when he
picked up the phone, I reintroduced myself and stated the purpose of
my visit. I received an unexpected response, which rather surprised
me: "Please, sir, do not phone me between 8 in the morning and 5 in
the evening!" How could he scold a visitor who had come from so far?
He had been so polite and warm in our chance meeting in Tel Aviv
just a few months earlier. Goitein then asked for my telephone
number. I dictated the number and the conversation ended.

But at about 5:30 p.m. on the same day the telephone rang in our
apartment and I heard Goitein's voice once again. "I am sorry that I
could not speak with you this morning. I am busy on an exhausting
research project and I must try to avoid disturbances during my work

day between 8 and 5." Then, Goitein asked if I had my family with me, and when I said that we were four – my wife, myself, and two girls (and in addition to that, my wife Terrie was pregnant), he answered: "My address is such-and-such Hamilton Street", adding, "please come for dinner on Saturday evening." Now his voice was utterly friendly and soothing. I was relieved. On Saturday evening we went to his house, and there we met his wife and mother of his children (whom he simply called "mother"). We were welcomed as friends by the elderly couple, and after dinner Goitein proposed to his wife to take my wife and children out to the garden, as he pulled me into his study. On his table was an enlarged photocopy of a Geniza document. He held it in his hand and said: "shall we study this document a bit? You have an advantage. These documents are written in Judeo-Arabic, your mother tongue, and you will certainly be able to help me decipher them". And again I was surprised: the greatest Geniza scholar in the entire world, asking me, who hadn't the slightest idea about medieval Judeo-Arabic, to sit with him on texts from the Geniza. I agreed of course, and we worked together for about two hours, during which time we managed to go through two or three lines of the document. He proposed that we visit them again on the following Saturday evenings and that way we could work together. And indeed we visited the Goiteins on Saturday evenings as much as we could.

In February 1975, our son, Nadav, was born, and Goitein called to congratulate us. About a month later he called again and asked if we would be home that evening. He said that he would come with his wife to congratulate us on the birth of our son. My wife and I were excited, since up until then the Goiteins had declined our invitations. Our apartment was in complete chaos, and we didn't have anything suitable in the refrigerator to serve such honorable friends as the Goiteins. I ran to the 24-hour supermarket, and bought whatever I could find. At the appointed hour, the doorbell rang and the professor and his wife arrived, the two of them dressed in their best clothing. They sat down, and a while later Goitein asked to see the baby. He held him on his lap, and suddenly I heard him say: "In the year 2000, Nadav will be 25 years old, and I will be one hundred, because I was born in 1900. Tonight is my 75th birthday, and I wanted to spend it with friends." Terrie and I were greatly moved at hearing him express such warm, intimate sentiments. In 1986, we came once again to Princeton, where I was a visiting professor until 1989. Goitein was no longer alive, having died in 1985 (they say that he died the day after completing the last sentence of his monumental work, *A Mediterranean Society*, to which I will return). In the 1988–1989 academic year, I was a guest at the Annenberg Institute at the University of Pennsylvania, directed by Professor Bernard Lewis. There I renewed my interest in the Cairo Geniza.

What is the Geniza? This is not the place to offer a detailed description of the Cairo Geniza, about the circumstances of its creation, about its discovery, or about the revolution it caused in the study of medieval Jewish history. I will make do with the main points: At the end of the nineteenth century, an attic was discovered in the ancient Ben Ezra synagogue in Old Cairo, filled with piles of hundreds of thousands of papers and fragments of papers, most of them in Judeo-Arabic (Arabic in Hebrew letters). The papers in these piles, which resembled a garbage dump, had been thrown there haphazardly, because of the prohibition in Jewish tradition to destroy a paper that has Hebrew letters on it. The great miracle was that most of these documents had been preserved for about one thousand years, thanks to Cairo's dry climate. The collection contained manuscripts by Maimonides and Judah Halevy, and by hundreds of other writers from the early Middle Ages. There were also liturgical and secular poems, as well as literary and theological treatises. All of these were important for reconstructing previously unknown ancient works. Besides the "literary" texts, the piles also contained tens of thousands of personal and mercantile letters, as well as fragments from merchants' logs and inventories with no apparent inherent literary or historical value. But in the eyes of historians of economic and social history, these documents were a veritable treasure trove. Quickly, scholars began reconstructing the modus operandi of the medieval Mediterranean market place, the movement of maritime and land trade, and the fluctuations of the prices of commodities. Likewise, we discovered things about daily life, family, education, and diet. All of these data were drawn from those same "documentary" texts (as Goitein dubbed them, to distinguish between them and literary works), which were sometimes only scraps. Goitein himself invested more than twenty years of his life toiling in order to summarize the knowledge that the Geniza documents provided (and still provide). In 1967 he published the first volume of *A Mediterranean Society*, and at the end of his life he completed the fifth and final volume (a sixth volume, of cumulative indices, appeared posthumously).

As a typical "jekke" (German Jew), Goitein went systematically through and documented every single discovery he made. He catalogued his material meticulously (the computer was not yet commonly used), and left behind dozens of boxes of indices and citations (known as "Goitein's Laboratory". I was fortunate enough in 1987 to be given a desk in a study at Princeton where a copy of this "laboratory" was kept, and for two years I sat with these boxes next to my desk!).

Goitein's six volumes are the foundation stone for the study of the "Geniza Society", in other words, of Jewish society in the Mediterranean basin, North Africa, and across the Middle East. This is a Judeo-Arabic society in the period of the golden age of Arabic culture, roughly between the tenth and thirteenth century, which saw the blossoming of some of the greatest Hebrew philosophers and poets of all times, including Shmuel Hanagid, Judah Halevy, Ibn Gabirol, Sa'adya Gaon, and Maimonides. The months I spent in Goitein's company in Princeton opened my eyes to the full importance of the study of the Cairo Geniza, and henceforth I had deep admiration for its scholars.

CHAPTER
16

STUDENTS AND COLLEAGUES

I spent over thirty years on the faculty of Tel Aviv University. I could skip over this part of my life and pursuits, dismissing it on the claim that it was "just my job" and that it had no particular intrinsic value. But that is not the case, partly because, alongside my professional and academic endeavors, I was called upon over the years by the media to discuss the looming questions concerning Israel and its neighbors – as if my expertise in Arabic literature gave me the authority to prophesize about the future. I always objected outright to such "prophetic" questions, explaining that all I could do, in the confines of my professional knowledge, was to interpret the past, at the very most.

When I returned to Israel from Oxford in 1968, PhD in hand, I had the good fortune of having a position at Tel Aviv University awaiting me. To be precise, I arrived in Israel approximately three months after the opening of the 1968–1969 academic year and began teaching in the second semester, in January or February 1969. The Department of Arabic Language and Literature, in whose founding I was to have participated, had been established without me. The highly respected Professor M.J. Kister, a scholar of early Islam, was brought in from Jerusalem to head the Department. Upon my arrival it was explained to me that I was the only full-time teacher in the department. The rest of the lecturers, Professor Kister included, worked on a temporary or part-time basis; even the department head held a half-time position. The first class I gave at the opening of the semester, on contemporary Arabic literature, was attended by fifty students, some of them adults (most of them Jewish teachers who had come to Israel from Arab lands without any academic formation, but also many Palestinian teachers from the Arab villages and towns). I did my best to take off from the literary texts and digress into the realm of literary theory, trying to make it clear to my students that their academic studies would require attention to the history and theory behind the material. The department's curriculum expanded in its first three years, and in 1972 we awarded Bachelors' Degrees to our first batch of students. We were very proud of these graduates, many of whom went on to teach Arabic literature in the Arab and Jewish sectors in Israel.

That year I was given tenure, and after that I was appointed head of the department. I held this position for over a decade, until a new generation of our graduates was ready to take over the administration and steering of the department. In 1975 I was made Associate Professor, and in 1983, I was awarded the new chair in Arabic literature, a position I held until my retirement in 2002. In my years of heading the department there was never a dull moment – within the university or outside of it: the War of 1973 and the upheaval it wrought upon Israeli society; initial contacts with Egypt; the beginning of serious contacts toward the signing of a peace accord beginning in 1977; President Sadat's visit to Israel and the attempt to foster a true peace and neighborly relations between the two countries, as much as possible. Although I was an outside observer and had no official role in the peace proceedings, I was often called upon for consultation. And indeed I spent a good deal of time on these matters – above and beyond the many hours I spent teaching, managing the department, and doing my own research, which is the very air that every scholar breathes (as they say, publish or perish). In those same years our daughter Avigal was born (in 1970) as was our son Nadav (1975), and I also occasionally took on additional jobs on in order to support my family of five with dignity.

In the 1980s and 90s, having been relieved of my administrative duties, I spent much of my time advising doctoral students in the field of Arabic literature. If I have anything to be proud of, it is these doctoral students, many of whom went on to become renowned professors at leading universities in Israel and abroad. Three of these PhDs eventually went on to head the Arabic departments at the Tel Aviv and Hebrew Universities, and about ten more of "my" doctoral students were hired for teaching positions at prestigious universities in Israel and the United States. Today these are expounding theories of modern Arabic literature to hundreds and thousands of students – according to their own understanding of the literature, but also, to a certain extent, taking from what they learned under my guidance. All of them emphasize the precedence of the literary text over any discussion of the content and, moreover, the importance of analyzing the overall structure of the literary text before making any thematic conclusions about it.

Another source of pride for me has to do with the great variety of "my" PhDs – gender-wise and ethnically speaking. Six of them were Palestinian-Israelis, and two of these were appointed to head the Department at Tel Aviv University during the 1990s. The Jewish-Israeli students also came from different ethnic backgrounds, both Ashkenazic and Sephardic. One student, Gabriel Rosenbaum, was appointed professor at the Hebrew University and was later chosen to head the Department of Arabic Language and Literature there. Recently he moved to Cairo to head the Israel Academic Center. I also advised, along with Professor Gideon Goldenberg, Dr. Shlomit Shraybom-Shivtiel on her dissertation on the history of the Academy of the Arabic Language in Cairo. Her thesis was published in its entirety by Jerusalem's prestigious Magnes Press. Another doctoral student of mine, Dr. Mahmoud Kayyal, published his book (also at Magnes Press), which began as a dissertation under my guidance, on the history of literary translations from Hebrew to Arabic in Israel and in the neighboring countries in the second half of the twentieth century. To my great joy, Kayyal filled my "slot" after I retired from teaching at the University. These students' books – published in Hebrew, Arabic, and English – have become an integral part of the corpus of research in their fields, and have been received enthusiastically in professional academic forums. I have mentioned just a handful of my many treasured students, with whom I have kept up excellent relationships even after the submission of their dissertations. I would just like to add that one of my students, Dr. Irit Getreuer, who in her dissertation on Naguib Mahfouz which she completed in the 1990s, analyzed the works of the great Egyptian writer from the period following the publication of my book, *The Changing Rhythm*, in a sort of continuation of my own work.

As for the faculty members from different fields whom I met in my years as a professor, I will mention just a few (some of whom have, in the meantime, passed away) who come to mind every time I recall my years at the northern Tel Aviv campus. First and foremost is Professor Andre de Vries, who was rector of the University when I returned from England. De Vries was a Dutch Jew, whose accent, manners, and worldview betrayed his origin. De Vries, an eminent doctor, moved from Jerusalem to Tel Aviv in order to establish and integrate the medical school into the surrounding hospitals (Beilinson, Tel Hashomer, and Ichilov). He spearheaded the expansion of Beilinson Hospital and the creation of its medical campus. De Vries juggled many tasks at once: treatment of patients, medical administration, academic administration and teaching, and administration of the entire University. His day began at 5 a.m., in the Gordon Street Swimming Pool, and sometimes he worked until midnight. However, aside from these "duties", de Vries did not neglect his own spiritual and personal enrichment. He regularly attended a weekly Talmud lesson (outside of the university), notwithstanding his being an utterly secular and cosmopolitan person. He also studied Arabic with astonishing persistence, even if his progress was slow, having so little time to spend on these studies.

No sooner had I settled into the Arabic department at the University that de Vries summoned me. He told me about his plan to require every student at the university to study Arabic, preferably spoken Arabic. Although I was skeptical about his proposal, I agreed to help him as much as he would need. This complicity was the start of a vibrant friendship between my big boss and me, which lasted many years. We went on frequent Saturday outings with our families to visit Arab towns, where he was invited by friends and colleagues, and I supplied him with Arabic literature to read, upon his request. In short, never have I met a person who so successfully managed his professional tasks while also leaving himself time for "personal enrichment", as he referred to his extra-medical activities. After his retirement, De Vries continued to volunteer, teaching a course for young Arab doctors, for which he drove on his own to Nazareth and back, even in his old age.

I also became very close with the pioneering generation of lecturers at Tel Aviv's Department of Poetics and Comparative Literature and at the Porter Institute of Literature. Professors Itamar Even-Zohar, Meir Sternberg, and Benjamin Harshav (the founder of the department and the institute) were my close friends on the campus for years; and my ongoing interest in literary and translation theory is largely thanks to them. Benjamin Harshav ultimately moved to the United States, where he teaches at Yale University.

Another professor whom I must mention is Moshe Gil. Gil, a veteran kibbutznik, began his academic studies at a relatively late age. After finishing his studies at Tel Aviv University he went to the University of Pennsylvania, where he specialized in the historical study of documents from the Cairo Geniza under the guidance of Professor S.D. Goitein. Upon his return to Israel he was appointed head of the Department of Jewish History, and over the course of his thirty years at the University, even after his retirement, he produced about a dozen thick volumes about different aspects of Jewish community life in the medieval Middle East, as reflected in the Geniza documents. It is difficult to put into words the amount of work that went into these books – the deciphering and printing of thousands of documents, in Arabic, Hebrew, Aramaic, and other languages, to make them available for future scholars. We became very close friends, and even after his retirement (after my own in 2002) we continued to get together and to read one another's writings (and given the sheer volume of his, I cannot honestly speak about much evenhandedness in our reading loads!). Twice I was asked to write in the weekend supplement of *Ha'aretz* about two of his epic works. I wrote these articles with an informative goal in mind; I wanted to explain to the average Israeli reader the importance of the Geniza and its scholarship in reconstructing a part of history that was not always apparent to the average Israeli. These articles and other pieces I wrote about the study of the Cairo Geniza aroused interest among many readers, and if I succeeded in making the public aware of Moshe Gil's exemplary scholarship, then I have done my job.

I made many friends at the University over the years and I cannot mention all of them. Among those who were not close to "my" field, I would like to mention Yehoshua Yortner, an outstanding scientist in the field of physical chemistry. He served for ten years as the president of the Israel Academy of Sciences and Humanities in Jerusalem and was in this position when I began my work as the head of the Israel Academic Center in Cairo, a subsidiary institution of the Academy. As the big boss, Yortner was aware of the difficulties faced by the director of the IAC and was always ready to help. His support of the Center and its directors stemmed not from personal motivations but from a touching awareness of the importance of the IAC and the need to allow it to keep running at full force even if the result did not always live up to our expectations.

My closest friends included many professors of the modern and premodern Middle East. First and foremost I would like to mention Israel Gershoni, a vigorous and innovative scholar who specialized in the study of Egyptian intellectual life and nationalist streams. Our friendship blossomed over the years in part due to our shared interest in Egyptian culture, and every time a book of his came out (in Hebrew or in English, and also in Arabic translation), I felt a great satisfaction as if I myself had written or helped write these books. He gained an amazing scope of new knowledge from the patient and comprehensive reading of unconventional sources. While writing this very chapter I received a copy of his new book in the mail, 500 dense pages long, about the construction of contemporary Egyptian national identity through monuments and memorial sites. I set the writing of this chapter aside in order to read the new book with the intention of reading the first pages – but after starting, I could not put it down.

Two other scholars whose main focus is Egypt are Professors Haggai Erlich and Shimon Shamir. Erlich's publications include a study about university and student life in Egypt, primarily between the two world wars, as well as other studies about Egypt. Erlich also researched contemporary Ethiopia and studied its language. His books and connections contributed greatly to our knowledge about Ethiopia, which is the country of origin of many Israeli citizens today. Shimon Shamir, for his part, is a profound researcher whose early works included a series of formative studies about the Egyptian intellectual class in the national and political context. In recent years, after spending several years in Cairo as head of the Israel Academic Center and Israeli ambassador to Egypt (and later in Jordan), Shamir was drawn to the subject of ecology and architecture, and he and his wife Daniella built a house on the Mediterranean coast, near Herzliya, combining ecological principles with Egyptian architectural and decorative arts.

Last but certainly not least of the Middle East scholars whom I would like to mention here is Professor Ami Ayalon, a scholar of the history and discourse of Arab journalism. His first book is an innovative exploration of the advent of the Arabic terminology of modern political life (terms such as parliament, law proposal, republic, etc.). Many of these are taken from terms coined by the Turks over the last centuries – in fact often Turkicized Arabic words. In other words, Ayalon's book observes how Arabic words were borrowed by the

Turks, given new meanings in Turkish, and subsequently reincorporated into the Arabic linguistic context with the new meaning intact. Two of Ayalon's books deal with the history of the Arabic press, and another deals with the advent of print and literacy in Palestinian Arab society in the days of the British Mandate.

And what of my own research? After all, without research and international publications, a scholar cannot survive in today's academia. This is not the place to list my books and other writings in my professional field. Suffice it to say that my bibliography includes monographs on two Egyptian writers – Naguib Mahfouz and Yusuf Idris – in which I emphasized the purely literary aspects of their works (language, structure, character design). In these books I adhere to the principles of the Russian formalist school of literary criticism – "to focus on the purely literary aspects of literature". The researcher of literature must focus on those devices that are intrinsic to the literary work and avoid, insofar as this is possible, using the literary text to look at social and political issues. That is best left to sociologists and political scientists. Likewise, I wrote a sort of introduction to the language of modern Arabic literature,[7] focusing on the language that shook itself loose of the linguistic-literary legacy of the Middle Ages to create a new language, suitable to the needs of the modern age.

---

7 *Genre and Language in Modern Arabic Literature* (Wiesbaden 1991).

CHAPTER
17

1988 – TWO EXPERIENCES

Toward the end of our extended stay at Princeton, at the end of the eighties, I had two moving experiences, about which I will tell briefly here.

In October 1988 came the sensational news of Naguib Mahfouz's winning the Nobel Prize for Literature. Those American newspapers that specialized in write-ups about prize laureates of all sorts searched their biographical dictionaries and histories of literature, but came up empty-handed, since the Egyptian writer was virtually unknown in the West. The public relations office at Princeton University sent out a press release saying that there was a visiting professor at Princeton who had written books about Naguib Mahfouz. Soon enough, the press ambushed my telephone line. All that day, until after midnight, I was busy filling in the blanks for these journalists. In all of my many conversations that day I emphasized two points. The first was that Mahfouz was an innovative writer who had placed the Arabic novel on an international level. The second point I emphasized was the writer's steadfast support of the peace process between his country and Israel. The last conversation, at 1 a.m., was with the editor of a San Francisco Chinese-language daily. He asked about the smallest of details, and I eventually had to ask him to let me go since I was very tired. The next day my statements appeared on the front pages of some of the leading US newspapers: *The New York Times*, *The Washington Post*, *The Philadelphia Inquirer*, *The Boston Globe*, and more. The only one who sent me a copy of his paper on that same day was the Chinese editor; but I couldn't find anyone at Princeton to read and translate the article for me.

The following day I wrote an article in Hebrew about the book, which I called "Very Egyptian, Very Human", and it featured prominently in the Israeli national daily *Ma'ariv*. I was sorry to be far from the Middle East in those exhilarating days (as an aside, a few days later an Arab-American reader wrote a letter to the editor at *The Washington Post*, complaining about the American press's hostile attitude to the Arab world: "even when an Arab writer receives the Nobel Prize, you ask someone from Israel about him", he wrote).

Mahfouz came out of the shadows into the bright light. All of his enemies and detractors in the Arab world now bowed down before him. I recall the many conversations we had in recent years about this subject: Why didn't the great Taha Hussein win the prize? And what about Tawfiq al-Hakim, who died in 1987? He would raise these questions every time the Nobel Prize was mentioned. I could recount more stories of jealousy and score-settling, primarily on the part of Egyptian writer Yusuf Idris (whom I admire greatly as a writer, but as a person he left me disappointed). Mahfouz himself maintained his self-control (at least outwardly). His speech at the ceremony in Stockholm, was read by one his colleagues because he could not attend in person. In his speech he stayed away from arrogant or provocative statements.

The second experience has to do with my first real foray into the study of the Cairo Geniza. In a previous chapter I described how Professor S.D. Goitein and I pored over Geniza documents at his home in Princeton, but up until 1985 I did not think to try my hand at this on my own. This is how the story went. I was a guest at the time at the Annenberg Institute in Philadelphia, where I happened upon a photocopy of a Geniza document. Upon first perusal I noticed that the word *targum* (translation) appeared over and over again. And since translation is my passion, I sat down, deciphered the entire document (which was written, as expected, in Judeo-Arabic), and showed it to my friend Mark Cohen, professor of Jewish history at Princeton University. Cohen called me from Princeton and told me that this document was unknown, but that it mentioned Yaqub Ibn Killis, a convert from Judaism and vizier at the beginning of the Fatimid caliphate in Egypt (the document was written around 980 CE). The two of us spent months working on the short document (only two-pages long), since it contained many errors in transcription. It turns out that it was written by a Jew who took part in the weekly *majlis* (study session) held by Ibn Killis in his magnificent palace in Cairo. The writer of the document notes the presence of Jews, both Rabbinic and Karaite, as a routine matter at the *majlis*; the anonymous Jewish writer also (subtly) scolds the vizier for making, and allowing the attending scholars to make, offensive remarks about Jews and the Jewish liturgy. In effect, this was the first instance of a Jewish document making explicit mention of the participation of Jews in the *majlis*, and it also provided us with first-hand testimony of Ibn Killis's insults and the reactions of the injured parties. The article we wrote was accepted for publication in the long-established American academic journal *Jewish Quarterly Review*. Cohen asked me to prepare a lecture on the subject for presentation on both our behalves at the conference of the Society of Judeo Arabic Studies, which was set to take place in Tel Aviv.

One would expect anyone interested in historical facts to welcome the discoveries this text revealed to us. It was for this reason that Mark and I had taken it upon ourselves to decipher the document and publish it along with an English translation and comprehensive analysis. And then came the moment of truth, I stepped up to the podium to tell the audience about the important text we had discovered. But instead of a sympathetic response came shouts of skepticism from two of the most distinguished Geniza scholars, attacking us furiously about the translation and our conclusions. Here and there it was possible to make some sort of response to their philological claims, but we were powerless at that moment to respond to the "ideological" challenge. The gist of the question that was posed to us was as follows: where do you get off saying that Jews participated in the *majlis*? Perhaps what is recounted in the document was no more than hearsay and not written by a first-hand witness. Our claim was that the participation of Jews in meetings of this sort is mentioned explicitly by quite a few Arab chroniclers of the period. Nonetheless, the document at hand was not written (in the part that we came upon) in singular tense, and neither the identity nor the name of the writer is clear. So there we were, in a standoff, with the great experts on the opposite side. However, practically on that same day, we received word of the discovery of an additional document that supported our claims. A brilliant American Geniza scholar disclosed to us that he had come across two additional pages in the Oxford Genizah collection, which he believed to be a continuation of "our" two pages (our document was located in the collection of the Jewish Theological Seminary in New York).

In the evening, Mark went to Jerusalem to look at the additional pages. A few hours later he called me and in his heavy American accent read to me the Arabic words at the top of the first page: "Upon hearing these words [of Ibn Killis and his scholars] I felt insulted . . . " In other words, the writer of the document was indeed among the participants of the *majlis*. Mark and I sat and wrote another article, translating and summarizing the two additional pages (which were indeed, so it turned out, a direct continuation of our two pages). *The Jewish Quarterly Review* published the two articles side by side in the same issue, in order to reflect the drama that had taken place between the writing of the first and the second paper.

Of course, scholars have the right to challenge their colleagues' conclusions. What was infuriating in this whole affair, however, was that, after all the documents were published, we heard no apology from our detractors for their rudeness at the Tel Aviv conference. This experience made me begin to doubt the willingness of some Jewish studies scholars, even the most eminent among them, to accept new material and to analyze it independently of their preconceptions about the relations between Jews and non-Jews.

I did not have much first-hand contact with Geniza texts after 1988, and indeed the unsettling feeling that accompanied the affair of the Ibn Killis document left its impression, positive and negative, on my academic consciousness.

In my thirty years at Tel Aviv University I had the opportunity to befriend some of the most eminent Geniza scholars, and alas I cannot mention all of them here. Of three of these greats, who were my friends at the University, I can say that I am still astonished at times by the productivity and originality reflected in the dozens of volumes they have published. I am referring to Moshe Gil, Mordechai Akiva Friedman, and Aharon Dotan. The first two were among Goitein's exemplary students. I should also commend the younger generation, most of whom were their students: Meira Polliack, Yoram Erder, and Shlomit Sela (who tragically did not live to see the publication of her impressive work on the study of the Arab echoes of the Maccabees story from the Book of Josippon).

When it comes to the study of the Geniza in Israel, I must also mention the great contribution of many American-born scholars, most of whom studied at Rabbinical seminaries in the US and later at prestigious American universities: Daniel Lasker, Joel Kramer, David Sklar, and my friend Mordechai Akiva Friedman, whom I mentioned above. Besides their colleagues at universities in Israel and abroad, all of these contributed greatly to deepening and expanding the paths of scholarship, whose main roads had been paved by S.D. Goitein.

Perhaps this "academic" experience did deter me, after all, from sticking my nose into the study of the Cairo Geniza in subsequent years, and from confronting – linguistically and historically – texts that need processing (and many of them do!). Nonetheless, my absolute awe at this "profession" has never ceased (calling the study of the Geniza a "profession" is perhaps not the precise term, since the Geniza contains a wide scope of texts of varying content and genre. Nonetheless, the Judeo-Arabic linguistic and cultural context demands a degree of expertise and "professionalism" – and indeed all of the scholars mentioned here are, if you will, first-rate professionals!).

During the 1990s I made a practice of writing, once or twice a year, an article for the general public having to do with the Geniza and its academic and literary fruits. These articles were sometimes published as book reviews on the subject of the Geniza. Most of these articles were published in the *Ha'aretz* cultural and literary supplement (where I also published articles and translations from my own field of modern Arabic literature over the years). I wanted to remind the Israeli reader, over and over again, that Jewish culture of the Middle Ages was to a large extent Arabized, and that the greatest Jewish luminaries over the course of 300 to 400 years wrote in Judeo-Arabic.

At this point I would like to linger for a moment on the concept of "Arab Jew", as I see it. I have a fundamental objection to the use of the expression "Arab Jew" as a general term for oriental Jewry, just as I disapprove of its use by Jews and Israelis abroad as a display of solidarity with these ethnicities, even when they do not know Arabic at all, in its contemporary or medieval form.

First: Not all oriental Jewish communities spoke or wrote in Arabic. The Jews of Iran and Turkey, for example, were not Arab Jews; these were Jews who lived in Muslim societies. Even modern Egyptian Jewry was, over the course of the twentieth century, more French than Arabic in its culture. Most of Egyptian Jewry was not literate in Arabic, nor did they speak it at home. Only the Karaite community in Egypt was Judeo-Arabic in the full sense of the term, and that community indeed generated writers and journalists who wrote in Arabic. Mainstream Rabbinical Judaism also produced excellent writers and journalists, but these wrote in French (for example, acclaimed writer Edmond Jabès and journalist Éric Rouleau – who were among the present-day editors of *Le Monde*) or in English (like the Cairo-born Jacqueline Kahanoff, whose writings were translated to Hebrew and published in Israel before appearing in English; and the Alexandria-born writer André Aciman, who published his memoir, *Out of Egypt*, in the United States).

Of the oriental Jewish communities, Iraqi Jewry (primarily that from Baghdad and Basra) is unique in that it adopted modern literary Arabic as its vernacular beginning in the first decades of the twentieth century. Thus the use of Judeo-Arabic, which these Jews had used until the end of the nineteenth century, gradually declined. The use of written Judeo-Arabic, with its incorporation of Hebrew and Aramaic expressions, had until then effectively confined the written text to the limits of the Jewish community and prevented direct dialogue between it and the general culture. Syrian and Lebanese Jewry used a mix of three languages (besides Hebrew and Aramaic, of course): literary Arabic, French, as well as Ladino. Yemenite Jewry, which was very integrated into the local Arabic culture, was "Judeo-Arabic" only in terms of the spoken and written language used for intra-communitarian purposes; this Jewry was quite disconnected from the elite culture of the surrounding culture, and very few of them learned classical or modern written Arabic. In that sense the Jews of Yemen, when they arrived in Israel, resembled all of Arab Jewry before the arrival of the modern era. They customarily read Rabbi Sa'adya Gaon's Arabic translation of the Hebrew Bible during their prayers and included it in the Taj (crown), their version of the Bible. However there is evidence that Sa'adya's translation (which was not necessarily written in strict literary Arabic and certainly not in Arabic letters) was not always clear to the Yemenites because it was written entirely in Arabic letters that tried to come as close as possible to classical Arabic. Evidence of this is provided by commentaries on Sa'adya's translation in the modern edition of the Taj. In other words, Sa'adya's translation does not fill translation's function of clarifying another text (the Hebrew Bible, in this case) but itself becomes part of the ritual.

My articles in *Ha'aretz* about the Geniza and about medieval Judeo-Arabic often provoked telephone calls and e-mail messages from friends (many of them highly educated and cosmopolitan) asking if I hadn't made a mistake when I wrote that the Judah Halevy's *Book of the Kuzari* or Maimonides' *Guide for the Perplexed* were originally written in Arabic (in Hebrew, the spelling of the words *ivrit* [Hebrew] and *aravit* [Arabic] are somewhat confusing, with just two letters being switched around). Hearing such absurd questions about the medieval Jewish world only served to reinforce my sense of the Eurocentric and severely lacking education of these interlocutors. And thus grew my desire to write again about the world of the Geniza – or more precisely, about the cultural context of the Judeo-Arabic experience.

S.D. Goitein writes the following in his *Jews and Arabs: Their Contacts through the Ages*, when discussing Judaism's contact with different cultures (Greek-Hellenistic, Germano-Roman, etc.): "Never did Judaism see such a firm and creative symbiosis as that which they had with Muslim civilization in the Middle Ages."

And why not continue dreaming – even in the current, disheartening, era in Arab–Israeli relations – that our children will see better days, and recall the words of Naguib Mahfouz:

> Doubtless, our two nations have known fruitful coexistence, in ancient times, in the Middle Ages, and in the modern era, while the periods of conflict and dispute have been few and far between. But, to my great sorrow, we have over-chronicled the moments of conflict a hundred fold more than we have recorded long generations of friendship and partnership.[8]

8 This citation is taken from Mahfouz's personal letter to me of October 12, 1978.

18

A MODERN EGYPTIAN SINBAD

The chapters of this book have been graced by many women and men who are no longer among the living, and many of these have left behind a void in my own life that is difficult to fill. As I write, however, I realize just how many other dearly departed friends have been etched in my memory. And yet, despite our closeness, they have not been given a proper mention in these pages. Perhaps their omission stems from the fact that they were not conspicuously situated at the important junctions about which I chose to tell. This must be the nature of autobiographical writing; not everyone who is worthy of mention is mentioned.

There is one person from among these "omitted", however, whom I cannot ignore as I tell my life story, even if his direct, tangible, influence on the course of my life was not great. I am speaking of one of the people I most admired, a person who came into my life around 1975 and with whom I nurtured a warm friendship until close to the time of his death in the late 1980s.

Husayn Fawzi was, in my opinion, the quintessential twentieth-century Egyptian intellectual. He was born right at the beginning of the century, in 1900, and died at a ripe old age in Cairo, the city of his birth, in 1988. Over the course of his life, Fawzi went through many stages in his career, research, and thinking. Although he was a restless person, he also had a great capacity to sit and learn. He left more than a dozen books behind him, all wonderful in style and worldview. Not all of these books are academic or professional, despite the fact that Fawzi himself was an academician through and through – serving, among other things, as dean of the faculty of natural sciences at the University of Alexandria during World War II. Fawzi had in fact founded this faculty, at the time when the blind scholar, Taha Hussein, one of the great intellectuals of modern Egypt, was rector of the new university.

Fawzi's books span a breathtaking array of subjects: history, literature, musicology, oceanography; they are all in their essence journeys – real and spiritual – throughout the expanses of Egyptian and human civilization. I read (or tried to read) his wonderful book *Sinbad's Ancient Discourse* as a boy in Baghdad, and as for the rest of his books (most of which include the name "Sinbad" in their titles – a mark of identification with the Arab popular cultural heritage and underscoring both kinds of journeys), these I read in later years once Egyptian Arabic literature had become my field. And the more I read the more my wonderment grew. In 1975 I wrote a long article entitled "Husayn Fawzi – Egyptian Writer and Scientist", which appeared in Aharon Amir's *Keshet* quarterly (and in subsequent years in English and Arabic versions). In this article I surveyed the bulk of his written works: his autobiography (*The Egyptian Sinbad*, 1968); his travelogue of the Indian ocean; his extraordinary account of Egyptian history (published in 1961, this book marginalizes the notion of pan-Arabism past and present, despite the fact that Fawzi was deputy minister of culture under Nasser); and finally, his work about the European Renaissance and the separation of science and philosophy from the church (1984).

Also an amateur musicologist, Fawzi wrote several Arabic-language books about classical western music in which he analyzed symphonies and other works by the greats of ancient and modern western music. These chapters had begun as talks on Fawzi's weekly special on Cairo Radio, which he presented for more than twenty years.

In 1975, while on sabbatical at Princeton University, I came upon Fawzi's complete works, together on a single shelf at the university library. I decided to read through them in order to write a study of his literary oeuvre (my 1975 *Keshet* article was one of the fruits of this sabbatical). Chance had it that just as I was immersed in Fawzi's writing, the head of my department informed me that Fawzi was coming from Egypt to give an informal lecture to members of the faculty and graduate students. I asked eagerly whether I could join in the meeting (our countries were still in a state of war, and I feared that my presence at such an intimate encounter might embarrass the speaker). The head of the department called him and asked whether he could invite a scholar from Israel to the meeting as well. The answer came forthwith: not only was the Israeli *allowed* to participate; but he – Fawzi – would like to talk with me personally at the end of his lecture. He even asked to cancel the dinner that was planned in his honor, to ensure that we would have the time for a leisurely conversation. And so the meal was canceled.

I came to that lecture hall and was amazed by what I heard. I did not expect a member of the Egyptian government to have the nerve to say what he said: "I was invited to speak on a subject of my choosing", so he began, "and I have chosen the subject of the High Dam" (meaning the Aswan Dam which was one of the applauded fruits of the collaboration between Nasser's regime and the Soviet Union). "Well", Fawzi added without faltering, "this is a typical fascist undertaking. What do I mean by fascist? When the regime strives and succeeds in creating a massive and arrogant project without taking into account the grave consequences. And what are these grave consequences?" Fawzi, a pre-eminent marine biologist by academic profession (I will write more about that later), then proceeded to go into the smallest details about the upheaval it had wrought on marine life in the great Nile, irreversibly altering the unique aquatic habitat that had arisen as a result of the natural current of the river. Moreover, the agriculture on both banks of the Nile would be totally changed. The dam's regulation of the tides would put an end to the seasons of high tides and flooding, which had been a great blessing for farmers for thousands of years as the rising waters from the Nile washed the fields and then returned to their regular course, leaving behind a layer of silt that fertilized the seeded earth and made possible the livelihood of its farmers. Fawzi added detail upon detail to his description of this disaster, in his opinion, known as the High Dam of Aswan – the pride of Nasser's Egypt.

What struck me even more was the fact that these jabs at the ultimate, practically sacred, symbol of the achievements of Nasser's regime, were made with complete freedom, and without any disclaimers such as: "What I am about to say should not leave this room!" No, Fawzi did not ask us to keep the contents of his talk to ourselves. In fact, he even quoted his own and others' studies supporting his data, and all this without reading or looking at notes. The questions following the lecture were equally biting, by which I mean that they did not tip-toe around the fact that here was an Egyptian criticizing Egypt to an audience of foreigners – Americans, and even an Israeli.

The hours the two of us spent alone after his lecture, were among the most exciting hours I have ever experienced. I say "the two of us", but to be precise I should say "the three of us", since his French wife, Diane, his life partner since the days of his studies in Paris, was with us all the time. She did not know English very well, unlike her husband who had complete mastery of the language. Thus the pace of the conversation was slowed so that she would not feel left out. It became clear that the Fawzis were close friends of Taha Hussein, the elder statesman of Arabic literature, and his French wife Suzanne. I was overjoyed to hear anecdotes from the house of the blind genius, as well as about Naguib Mahfouz, who was a friend of Fawzi's and his neighbor on the "writers' floor" at the headquarters of *Al-Ahram*. And then I heard the first truly joyful tidings from Fawzi's mouth. He told me that Mahfouz was among the great seekers of peace with Israel, and that he believed Egypt should make every sacrifice for the sake of peace and cooperation with its neighbor, Israel. This was before the publication of Mahfouz's interview with the Kuwaiti daily *Al-Qabas*, in which he directly and boldly endorsed peace between the two countries – not a superficial diplomatic peace, but a true peace. Fawzi took a copy of my book *The Changing Rhythm: A Study of Naguib Mahfouz's Novels* (1973) and promised to bring it personally to Mahfouz. Fawzi kept his promise, but fate had it that Mahfouz had been sent a photocopy of my book by a Palestinian professor at the American University in Beirut even before my copy reached him. When I met Mahfouz in his apartment on the banks of the Nile five years later, he showed me the photocopied version along with the original copy that Dr. Fawzi had brought him.

I confined my article in *Keshet* to a presentation of Dr. Fawzi's major writings and academic and public biography. I did not tell about our meeting at Princeton – for reasons of caution that later turned out to be unfounded. Thus, in the English version, which appeared two years later, I added an introduction in which I told in a nutshell about our meeting and the exchange of letters that followed it.

After the signing of the peace accords between Egypt and Israel, Dr. Fawzi became the first Egyptian intellectual to visit Israel. His first visit, which came at a time when I was abroad, was not because of our friendship, which had in the meantime grown stronger, but rather because he wanted to see the "other" on his own territory; indeed, Fawzi visited several more times in Israel. In 1988 he received an honorary PhD from Tel Aviv University. I was asked to write the text of his certificate, though to my great dismay I was once again abroad at the time of the ceremony.

Fawzi's death in 1988 was not without suffering. He was involved in a car accident in the last year of his life that left him bedridden for the months leading up to his death.

I had many opportunities to meet Fawzi in the 1980s – in Tel Aviv, Cairo, and Paris. On the last visit he had an apartment not far from the botanical garden (walking distance from the Sorbonne); I made a habit of spending part of my summers in Paris and part of my winters in Cairo, in part because I knew that this was his custom. On one of our many strolls near the Sorbonne and the Luxembourg Gardens, he stopped and pointed to an apartment on the fourth floor of one of the older buildings on the Rue St. Michel. It was in this apartment, he told me, that Tawfiq al-Hakim had lived in the 1920s and where the events of his book *A Bird from the East* (1938) took place. This was a small semi-autobiographical novel in which Muhsin, the hero and the writer's alter-ego, arrives in Paris at the beginning of the 1920s to get the full theatrical and cultural experience of the city. Al-Hakim's neighbor, who lived on the third floor, was a cashier at the nearby Odeon Theater. Muhsin falls in love with this young woman, Clothilde, and, to his great surprise, she submitted to him without much evasion. In fact, during the few days they spent as lovers, Clothilde was in a fight with her boyfriend, and she ends up returning to him at the end of their argument, leaving the enamored Egyptian despairing and bewildered at how in the West a woman can have sexual relations without being in love. And doubly surprising: how could her old boyfriend agree to take her back after she unabashedly flirted with someone else?

Fawzi had also been in Paris in those years, busy doing his PhD in biology, though his lifelong friend Tawfiq Al-Hakim filled him in as all the upheavals of his story of unrequited love unfolded.

Fawzi also pointed out the site of the biology laboratory where he had spent days and nights as a research student. The building on Rue d'École had been neglected and abandoned since the Sorbonne established fancy new laboratories in another part of town. He let out what sounded like a great sigh of nostalgia about those days sixty years earlier and about his mentors and friends in the lab, most of whom were no longer alive. Incidentally, Fawzi had come to Paris to do his graduate studies in science after completing his studies in Egypt at the Qasr Al-Eini School of Medicine specializing for a time in ophthalmology. "I am not Dr. Schweitzer and I do not wish to spend all my life in medicine", he told me on one of our strolls around Saint Michel: "I seized the first opportunity I had to go into research in the natural sciences, which was always my dream". And indeed, in one of his first letters to me, brought to me by an Israeli journalist who visited Cairo before I did, Fawzi told me that he had been invited by the Egyptian ambassador in Australia to give a lecture. He accepted the invitation, so he wrote to me, because Australia had a rare kind of coral about which he taught his students at the university and which he wanted to see with his own eyes while he was still alive.

In these pages I have not given a complete picture of the life and achievements of this amazing personality and talent. I tried to expand in those places that touch upon my life. I did not tell, for example, that in the 1960s he was editor-in-chief of the impressive literary monthly *Al-Majla*, which constituted a wholehearted call for freedom of expression despite its being funded by the ministry of culture. The editorials in this journal urged writers and artists to break free from centers of power such as the ministry of culture, the prize-givers, and the editors of the literary press. In one of these articles, entitled "Obligatory Material" (*al-muqarar*), Fawzi called upon his fellow university professors to abandon the *muqarar* system practiced in the Egyptian universities, in which students are required to read a standard and practically unchanging bibliography. In Fawzi's opinion, this system fossilizes the knowledge in the various professions and does not encourage the research and independent work that is essential for scientific progress.

As I wrote at the beginning of this chapter, all of his written oeuvre stands out for the element of the "search", but not just any search.

His explorations in Egyptian history from the ancient and Islamic eras present a picture that is not uniform. There are parts from which we can learn a lot and parts that might better be forgotten. In *Sinbad's Ancient Conversation* – in my opinion his greatest book and one of the heights of modern Arabic literature – he applies his great marine and biological knowledge to his study of the medieval travelogue (including the seven journeys of Sinbad). He deconstructs descriptions taken from sailors as well as from the imagination, and with a scalpel guides his reader in how to distinguish between the realistic and the fabricated. Although translated into English in Egypt about thirty years ago by a master translator, this book has sadly not yet been published in English.

CHAPTER
19

CAIRO – THE FOUR MASTERS

My first visit to Cairo was in January 1980. I was on sabbatical at Oxford University with my wife and three children when I received a telegram from Tel Aviv University notifying me that the Egyptian visa I had requested back in Israel had been approved, and that I could pick it up at the Egyptian consulate in London.

I hurried to get my long-awaited visa in order, and then reserved my round-trip plane tickets from London to Cairo, with a stopover in Athens. I spent several hours in Athens, on a cold and rainy day, and as much as I loved that city, I could hardly enjoy it due to the anticipation of finally reaching Cairo.

I arrived at twilight and made my way to my hotel, aptly named "Al-Nil", on the banks of the river. I settled into my room and went down to the Corniche (the promenade along the Nile that was erected with quite some fanfare in the 1930s). To my excitement, there was no divider between it and the river. To be in Cairo and to watch the waves of the Nile – this was a childhood dream come true. Had someone told me two or three years earlier that in another three years I would be in Cairo, as a civilian and unaccompanied – I would have said that he was hallucinating. On a theoretical level, I knew the city and its various neighborhoods – or so I thought. My emotional connection with the city went many decades back. It was then that I began reading the books of Tawfiq al-Hakim and other Egyptian writers, and, from my earliest childhood, the illustrated Cairene newspapers that came directly to Baghdad (*al-Hilal, al-Musawwar, Akhir Sa'a, al-Ithnen*). The names of the city's neighborhoods (Maadi, Shubra, Gizah, Zamalek, etc.) immediately conjured up vivid images of their inhabitants, and of the writers and artists who lived there. A colorful romantic connection was woven within me to Cairo and its streets. All of this was in the mid-forties, back in Baghdad.

Two decades later my relationship with the city suddenly intensified. In 1966 I began writing my dissertation at Oxford on the works of Naguib Mahfouz, the greatest of the city's natives in our time. When I began my research, Mahfouz had already written a dozen novels and many dozens of short stories, all of which took place in Cairo's neighborhoods, in particular in the old neighborhoods stemming from Medieval Cairo, which was established in the tenth century by the Fatimids. *Midaq Alley* and *Khan al-Khalili* were the names of his first two realistic novels, published in the mid-1940s to great acclaim. And above all there were the three volumes of his *Cairo Trilogy*, each of which is named after a neighborhood or street in Medieval Cairo. Over the course of three years I pored over a detailed Cairo street map to follow the comings and goings of the protagonists of these works. From tomorrow morning, I said to myself upon my arrival at the hotel, I will visit these places and see them with my own eyes, at long last.

My hotel was located in an area called "Garden City". This name had been given to the neighborhood at a time when it was covered with gardens and parks, but in the interim it had become a crowded neighborhood with not a blooming public garden to be found. But the Cairo magic filled it nonetheless, if only by virtue of its proximity to the bountiful river. But, again, this river was not what it once was, at least in my consciousness.

I am not a radical environmentalist, and I am aware that urban life (in particular in a crowded city of more than ten million inhabitants) cannot leave the environment clean and untouched. But on that same first outing, in a late evening hour at the Corniche, it pained me to see a man pushing a large cart full of garbage bags down to the river and nonchalantly dropping its contents into the water across from the Al-Nil Hotel, without a passer-by saying a word. I witnessed this kind of scene in the years following, in particular between 1995 and 1998, while living in Cairo in an apartment on the banks of the Nile.

At first I tried to speak with my Egyptian friends on this matter. They all agreed with me, but added that the situation was irreparable. The only person who took action was the writer Yusuf Idris, who, during my first stay in Cairo in 1980, wrote an irate full-page article in the daily *Al-Ahram* on the subject of garbage in Cairo, though not specifically about the throwing of trash into the Nile.

That very same evening I noticed an interesting phenomenon regarding the Egyptian "man on the street": the lack of distinction in their mind between an official representative of Israel and an Israeli tourist. In that period, preparations had begun for the establishment of the Israeli embassy in Cairo. There was a notice about this on the front page of one of the Egyptian daily papers. While I was walking and looking around, an Egyptian approached me and asked whether I was from Israel (how did he know?) and whether I spoke Arabic. When I said yes he began to lecture me about the kind of house that was needed for the Israeli embassy. He told me that he was a real estate agent and that he could show me some suitable houses. I answered that I was not there on any official business, and that I was a private tourist. This man could not fathom what I was saying, and with astounding insistence he continued to speak about prices and locations and sizes of houses that he had to offer "us" (with an emphasis on the plural case). Similar situations occurred over and over again, in different contexts, and I often found it difficult to make it clear to my interlocutors that I was just a civilian and did not represent any official authority. I will quickly add that many of the writers and lecturers whom I met on that same visit indeed knew how to distinguish between the "official" and the "private" in the Israeli context, and understood that I represented only myself. One of them, who worked at *Al-Ahram*, assuming that I might be short of cash, went so far as to pull out a 100 Egyptian lira (guinea) bill from his wallet at the end of our meeting and hand it to me, adding: "I know that you are traveling on your own account, so here are a few pennies that will make things a little easier for you. There is no need to return them quickly." I knew that 100 lira in those days were half or one third of his monthly salary. I refused to take the money, of course, but thanked him wholeheartedly.

I went up to my room in the Al-Nil Hotel and went to sleep for many hours after this long and tiring day. When I awoke the following morning I met both simple and educated Egyptians in the dining room at breakfast, including some of the hotel's waiters. A few of these told me about how they could not get married because of the economic situation, in particular because they could not find an apartment to live in. Later I read a number of Mahfouz's stories from the 70s and 80s, which described a similar situation – the impossibility of attaining an apartment – and its psychological repercussions for Egypt's young people. The events of the novel *The Day the Leader was Killed* (1985), take place on the day of Sadat's murder, but the background of the story is a couple that cannot get married because they cannot afford a house. They go their separate ways and each one of them experiences a personal tragedy.

At 10 o'clock I left the hotel and went to the square today known as Sadat Square, and there I encountered the elaborate buildings of the American University in Cairo. I approached and entered the central courtyard of the university campus. In the cafeteria I found male and female students sitting and talking. I was surprised to find, in this American institution which had been founded by Christian missionaries, female students dressed in traditional Muslim dress and male students with beards. I had not been aware of these phenomena even though I did know about the growing influence of religious and fundamentalist circles around the country, and about parts of Cairo, in which the religious influence was deeply and widely felt.

I wandered the hallways of the university and came upon a door labeled with the name of an Egyptian professor of Arabic, Said Badawi, one of the best in his field in the entire world as far as I was concerned. Thrilled, I knocked on the door, and then the professor opened the door and invited me in. I introduced myself, and to my surprise he knew my name. Taken aback, he told me that he didn't know that Israelis were already coming to Egypt as tourists. But then his face became friendly and he invited me to drink hibiscus tea (*karkadeh*, in Egyptian Arabic). He explained to me that this drink cleans the arteries and is healthier than tea and coffee, which are full of caffeine.

I bid farewell to this scholar with a positive feeling and a small package of his books and articles in hand. He was the first Egyptian professor I met in Cairo, and I wished myself many more such successful meetings. And let me say straight away: not always were my meetings with Egyptian colleagues so effortless. Some of them were trying to attain temporary teaching posts during their sabbaticals in the wealthy Arab states, and thus avoided meeting with Israelis; others didn't jump at the possibility of such a meeting because they had not yet come to terms with the peace with Israel.

I spent the rest of that day walking through the Cairo neighborhoods which I only knew by name; and the day ended with a meeting with Naguib Mahfouz in his apartment, as will be described later in this book. The experiences I had during this first visit – and in the many visits that followed – were so numerous and so varied that I could not possibly convey them all in these few pages. Each evening before going to sleep I wrote my impressions of the events of the day, and perhaps one day I will be able to dedicate a special book to them. In the meantime I can tell only briefly about my impressions from my first visits in Cairo, the city of my childhood dreams.

I spent entire days in the city's markets and neighborhoods, delighting in reading street names named after Fatimid kings and historical figures from the modern "Nahda" – the awakening to the cultures of the world. I admit that in parts of Cairo, particularly its modern neighborhoods, I found myself confused, since many of the important street names had changed since the 1952 revolution and the Suez War of 1956, replacing the original dynastic and cosmopolitan names with more "patriotic" names.

In what follows I will make do with my first encounters with people and phenomena surrounding my main fields of interest: Arabic literature and contemporary Egyptian academic life. More of these impressions are found in other chapters of this book (such as chapters 17 and 20).

Aside from Naguib Mahfouz, who was the main purpose of this visit, I met some of Egypt's great writers. First and foremost was Tawfiq Al-Hakim. Al-Hakim was president of the writer's union, and he had his own, spacious, room on the writers' floor of the *Al-Ahram* building (Naguib Mahfouz was given this room after Al-Hakim's death in 1987). Indeed it was Mahfouz who introduced me to him on my first visit to the *Al-Ahram* building (his room at the time was adjacent to Al-Hakim's). Al-Hakim recognized my name, since he had heard about me from his childhood friend, professor Husayn Fawzi (about whom I told in the previous chapter). I had much to tell him: how at age 12 or 13 I devoured his book *A Bird from the East* and how I searched for the areas mentioned in it upon my first visit to Paris, and how I would read his articles and short plays that appeared in the weekly *Akhbar al-Yawm*. Indeed, Al-Hakim's writings have a significant place at the foundation of my literary and spatial consciousness. A year earlier at Tel Aviv University I had organized a seminar in honor of his 80th birthday (the exact year of his birth – 1898 or 1899 – is unknown). Al-Hakim was happy to hear about the response to his works in Israel, and reminded me that his novel *Diary of a Country Prosecutor* was translated during World War II by Abba Eban, Israel's foreign minister for many years. I gave him copies of several articles I had written about his works and about related subjects, and he certainly read them (as will be told in the next chapter). He told me about the threats and curses he received on occasion in the mail because of his favorable attitude toward Israel, and gave me one such letter from an anonymous writer who curses the writer and wishes him that he be buried in the paupers' graveyard of Tel Aviv.

I will mention one of Al-Hakim's touching gestures: during my next visit to Cairo, a friend of mine, a radio presenter on Israel's Arabic-language radio, asked if I could find a book called *Song of Songs*, written by Al-Hakim in 1943, in which the author "dramatized" the biblical text of Song of Songs, placing the verses in the mouths of biblical characters such as Shulamit and Solomon. I passed this request on to the writer, but he told me that copies of the book had run out a long time ago. In my next visit at Al-Hakim's office, just a few months later, he greeted me with a cry of excitement: "I printed it for you!" "What did you print?" I asked. "*Song of Songs*", he answered. "I asked the publisher to reprint the book", he continued, "and here are two copies just for you. Here is something that will express the peaceful relations between our countries", he concluded, handing me the copies with trembling fingers.

Another writer the meetings with whom left me with a feeling of satisfaction was Yusuf Idris, a talented fiction writer and playwright from the generation that came of age under Nasser's regime. While the rest of the prominent Egyptian writers whom I mentioned up until now (Al-Hakim, Fawzi, and Mahfouz) belong to the liberal generation that sprouted in the 1920s and 30s, Idris, born in 1922, made his first literary steps at the beginning of the 1950s. And in contrast with the liberal generation, Idris was a revolutionary and a man of extremes. He studied medicine and worked in that field for a few years, but at the end of the 1950s decided to devote himself to writing. His many works succeeded in creating a new literary language that blended street language with literary language. Many of his stories were translated into Hebrew and to other languages. I personally was very interested in his work and wrote a number of studies about him, including a monograph entitled *The Fictional Language of Yusuf Idris* (Arabic, 1985). In the field of drama, Idris was very ambitious, trying to bring an "Egyptian form" to drama, in other words, to create a drama that would not be a continuation or imitation of the western drama. His plays saw theatrical success, but never – so it seems to me – was his dramatic work the height of his oeuvre. When it comes to his short stories, on the other hand, I am not alone in seeing them as great artistic feats, matched only by a few in the whole world. Idris dreamed of receiving the Nobel Prize, and when Naguib Mahfouz received it in 1988, Idris harshly criticized him, evidence that literary talent is not always accompanied by the sense of solidarity among writers. He died of a difficult illness in 1991, in his late sixties.

I hesitated whether or not to go meet Idris, since he was not at all sympathetic to Israel, and his past articles had cast hostile epithets at Israel. In the weekly *Roz al-Yusuf* in January 1978 an interview with him was published in which he lavished praises on my book *The World of Yusuf Idris* (Arabic, 1975), but adds his regret that it was done by an Israeli scholar. On one of my visits to the *Al-Ahram* building I saw his name on one of the doors. I asked the guard whether Idris was in his room, and he called up to him and told him that I was in the hallway. He came out of his room with open arms, and dragged me by the hand into the room. From that same moment I knew that my reservations had been unfounded. We became quite close and he would take me for rides in his old Mercedes around the city. One evening he hosted me for dinner at his apartment next to the Sheraton Cairo Hotel, to which he also invited his friend Salah Abd Al-Sabur, Egypt's greatest poet at the time. Three of my colleagues from Tel Aviv University, who happened to be in Cairo at the time, joined me and we spent an enjoyable evening into the small hours of the night. At one of our meetings in his apartment, he brought me into his study and, facing his bookshelves, announced festively: All of this material is for your use. You are the scholar I wish to be responsible for my entire oeuvre. Take what you want from my collection. I refused, of course; but he pulled out a collected volume of all of his plays and pressed it into my hand. When I got home I realized that this was a personal copy, which contained the writer's corrections between the lines and in the margins that were to be printed in the coming editions. I returned the copy to him, and he agreed to return it to the shelf with the dedication he had written still in place.

In my subsequent visits I tried to meet with Idris, but to no avail. His wife, Raga, told me that he was in bad health, but my impression was that Idris was hesitant about presenting himself as a "friend" of an Israeli scholar, while still carrying the title *Arab* writer with a pan-Arab audience that had not yet come to accept the existence of the State of Israel. For this reason I could not personally give him a copy of my book *The Storytelling Language in the Works of Idris* (Arabic, 1985), and had to pass it on to him through a mutual friend. That was my third book about Idris, in which I invested all of my academic energies.

All of these four, masters and friends of mine, passed away, one after the other. First Tawfiq al-Hakim died in 1987; a year later Professor Husayn Fawzi; in 1991 Yusuf Idris passed away; and Naguib Mahfouz died in August 2006 at the age of 95.

At the end of my first visit to Cairo, in early 1980, in the city's airport, I found a public telephone. I dialed Naguib Mahfouz's number in order to say goodbye. He asked about my impressions, and I said that it seemed to me that part of the Egyptian public was not happy about the peace between Egypt and Israel. Mahfouz answered without delay: "Those are communists and religious fanatics. While the rest of the Egyptians are absolutely in agreement with the peace, without which this visit of yours could not have turned out so well." I wrote these words down in my journal immediately at the end of the conversation. Later on I realized that the situation was not so simple and straightforward. The attitude to Israel in Egyptian public opinion is neither homogeneous nor stable. It fluctuates along with the frequent events in our region, and the media plays an important role, whether positively or negatively. Unfortunately, the negative has prevailed over the positive that had seemed apparent at the beginning of the process.

20

CAIRO – END OF THE CENTURY

When the idea came about in 1980 to establish an Israeli academic center in Cairo, I was, naturally, one of its enthusiastic supporters. The idea was that of my colleague, Professor Shimon Shamir of Tel Aviv University. He and I shared a great interest in Egypt, its modern history, its people, and its contemporary culture. Thus I saw the choice of him as the first director of the center as a timely decision. Shimon put much effort and resourcefulness into molding the form and content of the Center. A large apartment was rented in the center of Cairo, next to the Gizah Sheraton Hotel, in a building overlooking the banks of the Nile, and Shamir and his wife Daniella took care to decorate it tastefully and furnish it with an exemplary Israeli collection of books. A large table was placed in the center of the spacious library. Around this table sat (and continue to sit to this day) Egyptian students of Hebrew and Israeli studies, researching and writing their papers in the hours following their studies at Cairo and Ein Shams University. Two or three times a month, guest speakers on academic and literary subjects are invited from Israel to give lectures.

My wife and I were among the first guests to stay at the Center, which initially had two rooms designated for hosting guests from Israel, both researchers and students.

In its first years, the work of the Center was enveloped in an uplifting and optimistic atmosphere. The Center operated freely and with no need for security. Quickly, however, groups arose in Egypt that opposed cultural ties with Israel, and these groups launched an incitement campaign. In the opposition press, primarily a mix of

Nasserite sentiments and sensationalism, hostile articles were published and false propaganda spread about the Center, describing it as a branch of the Mossad planted in Egypt to spy and to implant Zionist propaganda in the minds of its students. Although this hostile propaganda was the farthest thing from the truth, some (though by no means all!) students stayed away from the Center, and the authorities heightened security at the Center as well as for its directors, fearing for their personal safety. In the 1990s it was decided to place an electronic screener at the entrance so that the workers of the Center would not have to search through the Egyptian students' belongings. Happily, to this day, no visitor or employee of the Center has been hurt, even if the incitement did not cease.

Three years later Professor Gabriel Warburg of Haifa University replaced Professor Shamir as the Center's director. Toward the end of Warburg's tenure I was offered to succeed him. I had to decline, however, due to family and personal reasons, even though the idea of spending three years in Cairo was very tempting. One reason for declining the offer was that in those days I was busy training young researchers at Tel Aviv University, and at the forefront of my considerations was the question: where will I be more effective? In Tel Aviv or in Cairo? Another reason was a more selfish one: I was completely consumed in the writing of a comprehensive volume on the role and transformations of the Arabic language in modern Arabic literature. I knew that in Egypt I would not have easy access to the sources and studies needed to complete my research (the book appeared in Germany as *Genre and Language in Modern Arab Literature*, in 1991). A move to Cairo at that time would perhaps have interrupted or at least slowed my pace of writing; and perhaps I would have lost momentum and interest and abandoned the project, which was so close to my heart.

Only after more than a decade did I take upon myself the directorship of the Center. In September 1995 I set out for Cairo (on my own, until the arrival of my wife a year later). I lived in a spacious apartment with a balcony overlooking the University Bridge (I "inherited" the apartment from my predecessor, Professor Emanuel Marx).

One of the leading factors that led me to accept the mission this time around was the fact that my children had grown up, and they could decide for themselves whether to stay in Israel or come with us to Egypt. As my departure for Cairo approached I was full of enthusiasm (if not excitement) since I felt there were great hopes on the horizon. Yitzhak Rabin was Prime Minister, and his government's policy was one that saw peace with Egypt and the rest of our neighbors as a valuable asset. Likewise, the Egyptian side saw Rabin's Israel as a peace-seeking neighbor. I heard encouraging details from Professor Marx about the growing cooperation between the Center and local academic institutions, students, and professors.

As I mentioned, I arrived in Cairo at the end of the summer of 1995, and began to feel my way toward solidifying the burgeoning optimistic mood. One of the first guests I invited from Israel at the beginning of my tenure was the writer Sami Michael, an old personal friend who was well liked by our Egyptian friends. One evening we returned to my apartment (where I was hosting Sami) and sat to hear the news from Israel. No sooner had we turned on the television when we learned that Prime Minister Yitzhak Rabin had been assassinated by an Israeli Jew at the end of the massive peace demonstration being held at the Tel Aviv Municipality square (today known as Rabin Square). From that same cursed moment, a harsh chill toward Israel began to settle in among the Egyptians. This change of climate was immediately felt. Student attendance dropped. Some of the Egyptian writers and scholars whom I knew, who before Rabin's assassination had begun to express an interest in visiting Israel, retreated and kept their distance from the Center, whether due to pressure from their superiors or from fears that were not always clear to me. In one such incident, two young Egyptian professors from the Hebrew department at one of the Cairo universities were preparing for a visit to Israel for an international seminar of Hebrew language and literature teachers that was to take place in Jerusalem, with dozens of participants from all over the world expected to attend. The two young people were excited in anticipation of the visit (they had never visited Israel and had never heard Hebrew spoken by native speakers), and from time to time they would approach me to clarify details regarding the upcoming trip, which was funded by the hosts. One day the two of them burst into the offices of the Center, their faces full of disappointment, and told me that their dean had summoned them for a conversation and forbidden them to travel to Jerusalem. I asked them how the dean had justified this cancellation, and they answered that his entire explanation could be summed up in the three words, "Netanyahu is bad". I pressed them further: didn't you make it clear to him that your visit to Israel would improve your skills in the language that you teach your students? And they answered that the dean's decision was final.

I wish to fondly mention two friends who joined me in Cairo for a year to help me run things at the Center: Rami Porat, an educator through and through, and Inbal Perlson, a doctoral student at the time, who after returning from her year of work in Cairo, died under truly tragic circumstances, drowning in a flash flood in the Judean Desert during a hike with friends in the valley.[9]

And as for the Egyptian students who persisted at the Center, they were wonderful in their vitality and academic curiosity. And I always took satisfaction in speaking with them and trying to answer their requests (such as searching for documentary material or ordering books from Israel). Not all of them, and certainly not all of their teachers, were supportive of the peace with Israel. Their visits to the Center and their explorations of Hebrew literature often softened their stances.

The hostility towards Israel would sometime brim over – often because of Israel's actions toward the Palestinians, though sometimes it was very difficult to identify specific actions of our governments as the source of the incitement. One such incident occurred upon the visit of the French anti-Semite Roger Garaudy in Cairo in 1997. Garaudy had recently published a book called *The Founding Myths of Modern Israel*. He came to the Egyptian capital on an honorary visit and to a warm reception by the literary and academic community in Cairo.

Garaudy, who in the 1950s was one of the prominent ideologues of the French communist party, had gone through several transformations in his ideological and religious life. From communism he went over to radical Catholicism, and several years prior to this visit had converted to Islam, becoming a devout Muslim. Of course no one has the right to challenge these changes in the spiritual life of the man. However the infuriating thing about this book, which is openly

9 The fascinating dissertation she wrote about the stories of the Jewish musicians who came to Israel from Arab lands in the first decade of the state was published as *A Great Joy Tonight: Arab Jewish Music and Mizrahi Identity*, only after her death.

hostile toward Israel, is the author's claim that one of the founding "myths" of Israel is the myth of the Holocaust. The Holocaust did indeed happen, but not only to the Jewish people and not primarily to them, he claimed. The Jews were one of the peoples harmed by the War, but the number of six million was a gross exaggeration, and all in all there were only hundreds of thousands of victims, so Garaudy claimed.

No self-respecting French publisher would publish this scandalous book, and the French intelligentsia, across the board, came out forcefully against it. Finally Garaudy found a short-lived publisher who agreed to publish his book in France.

Despite the scorn with which Garaudy was received in the West, his book was greeted most enthusiastically in Egypt. The book was translated to Arabic twice, and dozens of articles were written praising it. In Cairo a "Garaudy Celebration" was orchestrated by the writer Saad El-Din Wahba, a famous playwright and chair of the Union of Arab Artists, who to the day of his death in 1997 was a sworn anti-Zionist who vowed to destroy any display of normalization between Israel and Egypt. Taking advantage of the atmosphere of rage against Netanyahu's government and the clashes that accompanied the opening of the Temple Mount tunnel, Wahba managed to involve hundreds of intellectuals and journalists, among them leftists and liberals who in the past had displayed courageous stances against anti-Semitism.

A second phenomenon that upset me was the fact that the memory of Anwar Sadat has been almost completely erased today from Egypt's official history. Each year on October 6, Egypt celebrates the "October victory", what is known in Israel as the Yom Kippur War of 1973. The celebrations last for many days and all around the country the feats of the "heroes of the crossing" – meaning the crossing of the Suez Canal – are commemorated. However, in the media, which is largely controlled by the Nasserites, Sadat's name has been erased and one can even hear the claim that the victory was that of Abd Al-Nasser (who died, it is remembered, in 1970, three years before the October War). According to these claims, Nasser had planned the war and his generals carried out the crossing after his death, not under Sadat's leadership, but in spite of it.

The moderate leftist journalist, Abd Al-Sattar Tawila, one of the editors of the weekly *Roz Al-Yusuf*, was one of the only intellectuals to come out against such a blatant rewriting of history. He published an article in *Al-Wafd*, unequivocally denouncing the injustice done to Sadat, and criticizing the organizers of the central program for October 6 in which Sadat's name wasn't mentioned even once.

It is sad to note: on the walls in the Al-Dokki neighborhood where I lived in Cairo, I noticed a small and humble notice featuring a picture of Sadat in uniform, and under it the words: "Anwar Sadat, a hero of war and peace, gave his life for peace". It was signed "The Committee for the Commemoration of Sadat's Memory", in other words, a private unofficial association. The notice was pasted sloppily on the walls with cheap glue, evidence that it was a secret, almost underground, act. Truly unbelievable.

CHAPTER
21

AN ENCOUNTER WITH TAHA HUSSEIN'S GRANDDAUGHTER

My academic interest in modern Arabic literature and my engagement, in particular in my early years, with the world of Arabic literature, could not occur in isolation from the Arab–Israeli and Palestinian–Israeli conflict. Following my return to Israel, after completing my doctoral studies in England, I strove to distance myself as much as possible from political engagement. Truth be told, my choice of linguistic and literary pursuits did not stem solely from the love of those subjects, but also from the desire to avoid the influence of political and military events, and to stay as far away as possible from the urge to serve as a commentator on current events in the Arab or Palestinian context, always ready to explain or even foresee events. Although these intentions turned out to be in vain, when I did appear in public I always emphasized the disciplinary autonomy of my fields and their differentiation (from my perspective, at least) from fields such as contemporary history or political science. One of the reasons for this stance regarding literature was that I was absolutely fed up with what was called in its day "politically engaged" scholarship, meaning, a simplistic and self-righteous Marxist approach: the dialectical–historical worldview that saw the superstructure, meaning everything behavioral, intellectual, and cultural, as being determined by the base, or the fundamental class structure, in other words, by the power relations between employer and employee, between the exploiter and the exploited. This worldview never managed to explain most cultural or intellectual phenomena, including literature, on the level of concrete textual analysis.

Aside from the desire to distance myself from the realms of political ideology, or ideological politics, the emphasis on the autonomy of literature and linguistics in my academic life stemmed as well from my aspiration to treat the literature of my Arab neighbors with the respect it deserved. In other words, I did not want to treat this literary material as a means for understanding social and political phenomena in Arab society. Rather I strove to understand the problems of the contemporary Arab writer, who is torn from the outset between traditional literary conceptions (such as classical Arabic poetic theory) and modern literary concepts, in particular modern literary genres that the Arabic (and Hebrew, for that matter) literature of the Middle Ages was not sufficiently aware of (such as the social psychological novel, epic poetry, and drama in its various genres). The books and articles I published throughout my academic career, in particular throughout the last three decades of the twentieth century, dealt with contemporary writers from Egypt and from around the Arab world.

In my writing about Egyptian writers such as Naguib Mahfouz and Yusuf Idris, I studied their internal artistic development, which is not disconnected, of course, from their surroundings. From the 1980s onward, most of my studies revolved around the linguistic and stylistic dimension of contemporary Arabic literature. They often dealt with the acute *diglossia* that characterizes the linguistic reality in the Arab world and greatly influences contemporary Arabic literature, in particular in the novel and in drama. But my efforts to escape from the grips of the contemporary Middle Eastern political arena did not always work out, and perhaps one could say that I only truly found this autonomy in my academic writing itself. However the moment I came into contact with Arab literary circles, I could not but feel the intensity of the national hostility that existed on both sides. My meetings with Arab writers and critics often involved incessant and exhausting personal and nationalist tension. Yet some of the meetings I had with the writers from the neighboring countries were pleasant. At first I met writers, linguists, and scholars from the Arab world at the universities where I studied or taught in England and the United States (primarily Oxford and Princeton) as well as at dozens of academic conferences that took place around the world (for example at the International Congress of Orientalists in Paris in 1973).

After the peace accord between Israel and Egypt, the possibility presented itself of visiting Israel's past enemy's land and meeting its writers and intellectuals. In all of these places I found educated people capable of distinguishing between the Israeli as an individual (all the more so if this particular Israeli came from the Arab world), and Israel as a rather disliked political entity. I forged warm friendships with a few of these, and we could spend hours in fascinating conversations about literature and life. We did not often succeed in convincing one another of our mutually exclusive views about the issues of the hour, yet nonetheless we remained friends. Some of these friendships were made possible by the fact that my writing about Arabic literature is not hostile to this literature; it is a literature that I love and that played a formative role in my youth. And indeed, the eminent Egyptian writer, Dr. Husayn Fawzi (1900–1988), when asked by the Cairo daily *Al-Akhbar* in 1979, on the occasion of the signing of the peace accord between Egypt and Israel, why academics in Israel rush to study and write about Arabic literature, immediately answered that the world has a long tradition of academic research for its own sake, and in that way the universities in Israel are no different from the universities in the advanced nations. However not all, not even most, of the Arab intellectuals and literary critics, shared this view. The Egyptian literary critic, Sabri Hafez, who has served for several years as a professor of Arabic literature at the University of London, wrote a series of malicious articles reminiscent of the extremist Nasserite propaganda, in which he accused Israeli scholars, among them the late David Semah and myself, of being "academic weaklings" in the service of Zionist propaganda, without citing even one line of our writings to support his claims.

Somewhat less hostile was the well-known Egyptian journalist and critic Raga Al-Naqash, who in 1978 published a long article in the Emiratian monthly *Al-Doha* (of which Al-Naqash was editor in chief). The article was written as a response to the publication of my book *Language and Theme in the Short Stories of Yusuf Idris* (1976), an anthology of short stories by the Egyptian writer preceded by a long introduction in Arabic about the art of this writer. Idris himself was overjoyed upon his receipt of the book, and emphasized, in particular in an interview published in the weekly *Roz Al-Yusuf* a short time after the appearance of the book, how impressed he was with the stylistic-linguistic analysis of his stories. But Raga Al-Naqash could not stand silently by and hear the praises that his friend Yusuf Idris heaped upon it. He did nonetheless open the above-mentioned article with exaggerated praises for the expert critique of the "Israeli critic", but at the end Al-Naqash's praises transform into a warning. This researcher, says Al-Naqash, is no more than a cog in the evil machine whose purpose is to understand our weak points so that the Zionist establishment may continue to oppress us. In the final passage of his article, Al- Naqash writes: "To conclude, I wish to linger on a small sample of Israeli criticism of Arabic literature. This example will make it very clear to us how literary analysis can lead to social and political conclusions. The study written by the eminent critic Prof. Sasson Somekh, about the works of Yusuf Idris, points to the phenomenon of the multiplicity of contrastive expressions such as "only" and "but" in the last phase of Idris's works" [and then he brings examples from this analysis]. "This text is chosen by the Israeli", continues Al-Naqash, "so that he may conclude from it not only the phenomenon of the 'but' expressions and the like, but derive from it a generalized social implication. And thus he writes: 'The sequences of "but"-"only" sentences reflect a world in which uncertainty and incoherence reign, shedding light upon the general meaning of story-telling in this phase of Idris's works.' Thus is the analysis of the Israeli critic – a punctilious analysis, an analysis whose implied meaning cannot escape the observant eye". However this ostensible implication of mine elaborated upon in Al-Naqash's article could have been shown to be unfounded had Al-Naqash also cited the sentences immediately following, in which I write that these linguistic-literary phenomena are a common style in contemporary world literature and are not limited to the writing of this particular Egyptian writer. His approach, basically an attempt to attribute to every Israeli scholar a hostile stance ostensibly representing the desires of the Israeli regime, caused me (and others) more than a few media altercations over the years, particularly after the signing of the peace between Israel and Egypt.

I have already written about some of my moving encounters with the most important writers in Cairo and Alexandria, but I would like to tell about two additional incidents that at first seemed to indicate the realization of a beautiful dream, but that ended unpleasantly. The first incident occurred in Cairo, at the time of my first visit to Egypt in January 1980. Among the Egyptian writers I met on my first visit in Cairo was Tawfiq Al-Hakim, the most prominent Egyptian writer in those days, an eminent playwright and central literary figure for decades. I had already studied his works in my high school in Baghdad, and what I hadn't learned at school I read eagerly at the municipal library in Baghdad. His many books, in particular those describing the years of his youth in Paris, captured my imagination as a young man. In 1980 Tawfiq al-Hakim was president of the Egyptian Writers' Association, and one of the leading advocates of peace and reconciliation with Israel. My first meeting with him moved me deeply; here I was, after decades of wars and estrangement, shaking the hand of one of the cultural heroes of my youth. He met me in his spacious office on the writers' floor of the *Al-Ahram* building, and graciously accepted two articles that I had published in literary journals about his dramatic and fictional language. We discussed current events and the end of the wars between our two countries, and he pulled out of his drawer a letter scribbled in the handwriting of an Egyptian lawyer cursing the writer about his sympathetic stance toward the peace process, and wishing him to be buried in "the Jewish paupers' graveyard" in Israel because of his "treachery". Al-Hakim went on to tell me that this was not the only letter of its kind, and let me keep the letter in its stamped envelope.

Upon my second visit in Cairo, a few months later, I stayed in the erstwhile majestic Al-Nil Hotel, whose convenient location attracted many of the visitors from Israel. An Israeli friend also staying at the hotel told me that Tawfiq al-Hakim's famous literary salon met there every Friday morning, in the hotel lobby. And indeed, on that Friday I left my hotel room and saw Al-Hakim's circle gathered as usual. As I passed by the lobby, I was spotted by Chief Justice Ashmawi, a fascinating person and one of Al-Hakim's friends, whom I had met just a few days earlier and who was a regular participant in "Al-Hakim's Salon". He called out to me. I walked over and sat next to him in the last row. However Al-Hakim, who sat in the center of his friends, some forty or fifty men middle-aged and older, insisted that I come and sit beside him. He introduced me to those gathered and mentioned that he had read the studies I had given him some time ago and had found their approach interesting. I was thrilled, but at the same time I could detect the cold reaction and lack of enthusiasm on the part of the other participants. None of them responded to Al-

Hakim's words. Later Justice Ashmawi explained to me that most of the members of the circle were civil servants or journalists from the pre-1952 regime. They had lost their stature with Nasser's rise to power, and still had the fear of his regime seared in their hearts even though the "Ra'is" was gone, never to return. At the end of the meeting I bade Tawfiq al-Hakim farewell and went on my way. After my return to Israel I began to receive news clippings from Egyptian friends from the daily *Al-Gumhurriya*, featuring letters from some of the participants in the salon criticizing Al-Hakim for "flirting" with some of the "unwanted guests" from Israel. Disgusted, Al-Hakim responded, also in *Al-Gumhurriya*, that he believed that there will be full reconciliation with Israel before the resolution of the Palestinian problem. When I visited Cairo for the third time, I was informed that the salon had stopped meeting due to friction between its participants. I do not know if I should regret my chance participation in this weekly gathering, about which I had heard so much. In any case, I don't believe I deserve credit or blame for the break-up of this literary salon.

The second incident took place far from the Middle East, a few years before the signing of the peace with Egypt, and before I had the chance to visit that country. In 1975, while a visiting professor at Princeton University, I taught a course on Arabic literature. At one of the meetings of my seminar, a dark and attractive young woman appeared whom I had not met before. At the end of the class she came up and cordially introduced herself as Mona Al-Zayyat. In our quick conversation it became clear to me that she was the daughter of Muhammad Al-Zayyat, who was Egypt's foreign minister under Nasser, and of Amina, Taha Hussein's daughter. I faltered and stuttered, since Taha Hussein (1893–1973) had been the hero of my youth, the greatest writer and quintessential twentieth-century Arab intellectual. Taha Hussein lost his vision in his childhood but succeeded in overcoming his handicap and becoming the "Dean of Arabic literature". In 1951, with the victory of the popular Wafd Party in the elections, Hussein was appointed Minister of Education and spearheaded compulsory education in his country. I told Mona about the great admiration I felt for her grandfather and invited her to continue participating in my course, promising that I would devote one of the lessons to Hussein's literary heritage. We ran into one another occasionally in the hallways of Jones Hall where the

143

Department of Near Eastern Studies was located, and in every such meeting we exchanged friendly words. I told her that her grandfather had visited in Jerusalem, apparently in 1943, and had been a guest at the Hebrew University. I didn't notice any reservations on her part or desire to distance herself from me. Although our meeting was superficial and passing, it both amazed and thrilled me.

One day, as I was standing reading the notices on the bulletin board of the department, I heard the voice of the late professor Morroe Berger, one of the veteran professors at the university, conversing with a large man, who I immediately identified as Mona's father, who was then, as far as I remember, Egyptian ambassador to the UN or in Washington. When Berger saw me he said out loud to his companion: "Here is someone who can help us." They approached me and Berger introduced me to Dr. Al-Zayyat. Al-Zayyat told me that his father-in-law, Taha Hussein, had left behind an unfinished novel, and that now, some two years after his death, the family wanted to publish the material as a book, but that it was incomplete. I asked the name of the book. *Beyond the River*, answered Al-Zayyat. I immediately recognized that title, since chapters of it had appeared around 1947 in the monthly *Al-Kitab Al-Masri* which was edited by Taha Hussein. (This was a prestigious literary monthly, published by the local Egyptian branch of Gestetner duplicating machines, which was owned by the Harari brothers. It ceased to appear in 1948, with the outbreak of war in Palestine, I presume because of the fact that the publishers were Jewish.) Then Al-Zayyat recognized something foreign in my English accent and asked where I was from. I told him that I was an Israeli born in Baghdad. Immediately the man fell silent and didn't say another word. A few days later I met Professor Berger, and he conveyed to me that Al-Zayyat had been greatly insulted by our chance meeting, and extremely annoyed that the department in which his daughter, Mona, was studying counted among its teachers an Israeli teaching Arabic literature. And so this friendly encounter also ended in a sad way. I did not see Mona again, as she finished her studies at Princeton and went on to another place. Some years later an Israeli colleague who had met her somewhere in the U.S. conveyed Mona's regards to me. Once again I was moved. I had no luck tracking her down during my many visits to Egypt during the eighties, and she did not make any apparent efforts to get in touch with me.

22

NAGUIB MAHFOUZ – THIRTY YEARS OF FRIENDSHIP

When in the winter of 1966 I began to write my dissertation on the novels of Naguib Mahfouz, I did not imagine that things would turn out as they did: that he would be recognized as the greatest modern Arab writer and that he would receive the Nobel Prize. In 1966 Mahfouz was already 55 years old, and was considered an important and prolific, even central, writer, but not *the* Arab writer. Taha Hussein, the blind genius, the eminent playwright Tawfiq al-Hakim, and a long line of fiction writers and poets in Egypt and outside of it, were better known than he was. Mahfouz himself was regarded at the time as the founder of the modern realistic-naturalistic novel; and in 1961, when he reached the age of 50, he was written about, interviewed, and photographed with much interest. But it was inconceivable in those days that peace would be established between the writer's country and my country, Israel; that I would have the chance to visit Egypt and even spend three years there, to get to know the writer from close up, to spend mornings and evenings in his company. I did not dare believe that a friendship would form between us, one that would last for several decades.

Even as a teenager, I had been familiar with the name Naguib Mahfouz. I first heard of the Egyptian novelist in 1949 in Baghdad; he had recently completed two important novels, *Khan al-Khalili* (1946) and *Midaq Alley* (1947), named after the colorful, ancient back streets of Fatamid Cairo. A circle of very young Iraqi writers with whom I kept company in mid-century was divided over the question of Mahfouz's place in Arabic literature. Some saw him as a serious novelist and an impressive "sociologist"; others dismissed him because they thought he was not modernist enough. His writing tended towards nineteenth-century European naturalism; but in the middle of the twentieth century, so claimed his detractors, many decades after Joyce and Proust, there was nothing remarkable in writing realistic-psychological novels. I sided with the detractors, even though I had not read his works; perhaps I had glanced through them, but I had not actually finished a single one. My one great love then was modern poetry. I was about sixteen years old; these were my final days in Baghdad.

After I arrived in Israel in 1951, I lost contact with Arabic literary life, and for the next few years I gleaned only tidbits of information about famous writers and major innovations. In 1955, I read Mahfouz's *Beginning and End*, which first appeared in Cairo in 1951 and was reprinted in Israel four years later. I cannot say that this novel captured my imagination. In those days I was a true believer in literary commitment and even more strongly in revolutionary activity of the orthodox-Marxist sort. I felt that revolutionary passion was lacking in this novel. Mahfouz described Egyptian society's lower and middle classes, identifying with the oppressed, but without pointing to the source of oppression – capitalist and colonialist exploitation. I was disappointed not to find a "positive hero" symbolizing the "world of tomorrow". From my left-wing perspective, Mahfouz was not much of a cultural hero; he had definitely not attained a place of honor in the pantheon of our literary idols, reserved for luminaries such as Gorky, Brecht, Anderson-Nexoe (the Dane), Aragon, Neruda, Hikmet, and so on.

During my first years in Israel, I could not follow what was taking place in Arabic literature, including the great advance in Mahfouz's stature after the publication of *The Cairo Trilogy* and his winning the Egyptian National Prize in 1957. I had no knowledge of the publication of his allegorical novel *Children of Our Alley*, which was serialized in the Cairo daily *al-Ahram* in late 1959. Nor was I aware of the virulent attacks leveled against this work, even before the serialization was completed, in Islamic circles (especially by certain sheikhs at al-Azhar theological college). Their claim was that the novel insults the Prophet Muhammad, as well as other prophets, by presenting them as crude, licentious thugs. (Fifty years later, the novel has not come out in book form in Egypt; but there is a Lebanese edition of it.)

In October 1965 I was admitted as a doctoral candidate in the field of Arabic literature at Oxford University. As I recounted in a previous chapter, the first encounter with my future adviser, Dr. Muhammad Mustafa Badawi, was a turning point in my career. Badawi had recently arrived in England from Alexandria, where he had lectured in English literature. As our meeting approached, I was overcome by apprehension. How would an Arab professor relate to an Israeli? Why should he agree to accept me as one of his students in Arabic literature when my studies (in Tel Aviv and Jerusalem) had concentrated on Hebrew and general linguistics? In which language should I converse with him: colloquial Arabic, formal Arabic, or English?

Once inside Badawi's modest office, my fears vanished. We spoke a mixture of English and Arabic. When I mentioned that I was an Israeli, he responded, "Who asked you?" When I added that I had previously majored in linguistics and not in Arabic literature, Badawi replied with a twinkle in his eye, "Linguistics comes in handy". He suggested Mahfouz as a subject for my dissertation (modern Arabic poetry would have been my first choice). Not very enthusiastically I promised to look into it, and then walked over to the library at the School of Oriental and African studies to borrow the volumes of *The Cairo Trilogy*. I immersed myself in its 1500 pages. When I finished reading, I had found a topic.

The *Trilogy* was, for all intents and purposes, a continuation of Mahfouz's "social" works on Cairo; but in contrast to his earlier novels, which I thought "static", the *Trilogy* flowed with pulsating energy. It wove a tale around three generations extending from 1917 to 1943, the years in which Cairene society went through a staggering metamorphosis from a "medieval" patriarchal society to a new activism-oriented generation that included communists and Muslim radicals. To a great extent the *Trilogy* resembled the family saga of western literature, especially Thomas Mann's *Buddenbrooks*, a book that undoubtedly influenced the author. What impressed me most was the cadence, the rhythm that speeded up the longer we accompanied the characters in time. This tempo is felt not only in the plot structure and the characters' personalities, but also in the language. For someone trained in linguistics, I was attracted, indeed hypnotized, by this stylistic feature, namely the correlation between the rhythms of reality and the linguistic texture of the work. I devoted many years to studying it. *The Changing Rhythm* was the title of my book on Naguib Mahfouz, based on my dissertation and published in Holland in 1973.

While I was writing my dissertation, the Middle East was shaken to its roots by a fierce storm. The Six-Day War erupted in June 1967, and in its aftermath Arab messianic nationalism, in its Nasserite guise, began to wane – just as Jewish messianic nationalism in its *Gush Emunim* or "Greater Israel" manifestations began to emerge. I was nestled in a gray, drizzly English town, Oxford, studying the novels of an author who hailed from a country that my people were bitterly engaged in fighting, overpowering, and, to my dismay, humiliating. What am I doing here so far away? I asked myself. Why am I dealing in stylistic complexities and fictional meanderings, when in my homeland a violent conflict rages that for better or worse will determine our future?

And what of "my" author, Naguib Mahfouz? What are his political views? What is his attitude toward Israel and Israelis? How would he react if he heard that an Israeli was doing research on his novels? At that time, Mahfouz rarely expressed his views on political issues. When he did speak out, one could not differentiate him from other Arab intellectuals, none of whom desired, or dared, to challenge the nationalist tide. Studying Mahfouz's works written at the zenith of the Nasserite years, I detected shadows of discontent and a sense of strangulation stemming from a profound distaste for any type of dictatorial rule and one-party government. But I found nothing to suggest that he actually opposed the Ra'is's policy vis-à-vis Israel. For this reason, and out of a desire not to place him at risk (lest he be accused of contact with the enemy), I refrained from writing to ask him questions about his life and work. British friends of mine who frequently traveled to Egypt were willing to relay some sort of message, but I resisted the temptation.

Only after I had completed my doctoral thesis, and another catastrophic war had bloodied our two countries in 1973, did I begin receiving information about Mahfouz's "unorthodox" political views. Immediately following the Yom Kippur War, Mahfouz made an extraordinary declaration about war and peace that *al-Ahram* published. He called for a decisive focus on domestic, economic, and scientific development and charged that the "financial assets" available for this work were "piling up in foreign banks". Even before the war, in April 1972, Mahfouz had participated in a symposium under the auspices of *al-Ahram* that included Mu'ammar Qaddafi, then the young and irascible leader of Libya. Mahfouz and the veteran authors Tawfiq al-Hakim and Husayn Fawzi used such terms as "negotiations" and "peace" with reference to Israel. This infuriated Qaddafi, who apparently demanded an apology from Muhammad Hasanein Haykal, the editor of *al-Ahram*. It is worth quoting a few sentences from Mahfouz's description of this remarkable episode, written twenty years after the event:

> If war is not an option [I said]. We must choose a different path, the path of negotiations. We find ourselves in a no-war-no-peace situation that has no parallel in history, and its consequences may be far more disastrous for us.
> Qaddafi replied: "We may forgive you for what you have just uttered. The Arab leaders' sluggishness certainly encourages defeatist ideas like these!" Haykal intervened in an attempt to change the subject. . .

In a 1975 interview published in the Kuwaiti newspaper *al-Qabas*, Mahfouz expressed himself in an exceptionally outspoken manner. One of his statements that particularly enraged many in the Arab world's elite was that peace is more important than land, and that land could even be surrendered in exchange for peace.

Following the torrent of criticism directed against him, Mahfouz began softening his formulations, expressing himself in a way that would not offend his Arab readers, but neither did he alter the essence of his vision nor apologize for any of his statements. It comes as little surprise, then, that with the start of the peace process, after Anwar el-Sadat's sudden visit to Israel in 1977, and through the signing of the Camp David agreement, Mahfouz was counted among the most ardent proponents of these accords. Later, Arab opponents of a settlement with Israel charged that his support of Sadat's peace initiative was in keeping with his "innate submissiveness", which prompted him to follow the leader, any leader, and give him support. In defense, he replied:

The reverse is true. In fact, it was Sadat who supported me. My attitude towards negotiations was common knowledge even before Sadat came to power and before he accepted the principle of a diplomatic solution. . . . When I announced that we must initiate talks, I did anticipate being bitterly denounced. Yet I never wavered from my position because I believed that first and foremost it was an Egyptian and Arab interest to achieve peace; and I knew that the War of Attrition [between Egypt and Israel from 1968 to 1971] had been sheer nonsense. Prolonged military confrontation . . . will impoverish our resources and strength, while retarding our march to civilization by at least a hundred years. Why in the world should we not seek peace?

Peace with Israel was a fundamental principle from which Mahfouz would not budge, despite the ostracism and scathing condemnation he suffered for several years. Nevertheless, he was also capable of criticizing Israel during the wars in Lebanon (1982, 2006) and the Intifada. But he remained unshaken in his dream of sound neighborly relations and in his criticism of those who dreaded peace. In one of his pronouncements he declared,

> If Israel has a literature, I will read it and judge for myself if it is good or bad. But there are those who fear this and claim "If we have commercial relations with Israel, then she will overpower us; and if Israel introduces her culture, she will destroy us". [I say] these people have lost their sanity, their intellectual courage, and their self-confidence . . .

In 1973, when the English version of my study of Mahfouz appeared in Holland, I asked my publisher to send a copy to his address at *al-Ahram*. For some reason he never received the book. But a Palestinian professor photocopied the entire book at the American University in Beirut and sent it to him. I learned about this from an interview between Mahfouz and the Egyptian novelist and journalist Gamal al-Ghitani, published in the Baghdadi newspaper *al-Gumhuriyya*:

Recently, Professor Muhammad Yusuf Najm handed me a photocopied edition of a scholarly work by a lecturer from Tel-Aviv University named Sasson Somekh. This is by far the most serious research carried out on the *Trilogy*. The scholar deals with the different critical appraisals regarding this work, and arrives at the conclusion that at the base [of the *Trilogy*] is Man versus Time. The truth is that I was amazed at the researcher's accuracy and profound understanding. This shows us the extent to which [the Israelis] are interested in what is happening on our side . . .

Naturally, I was deeply moved. It was evident that this question in the Iraqi paper was "planted", as it appears at the end of a long series of questions. I was gratified to notice at the opening sections of the interview a few expressions which I often used in *The Changing Rhythm*, e.g., "The epoch's rhythm" (*iqa' al-'asr* in Arabic). A recently published book by Mahfouz, *Tales of Our Alley* (1975), is referred to in the interview as an example of Mahfouz's "new rhythm".[10]

In 1977, following Sadat's historic visit to Jerusalem, Israeli journalists began visiting Egypt and meeting with politicians, artists, and writers. Several of these journalists were themselves well-known Israeli writers, for example the poet Haim Gouri and the novelists Aharon Megged and Yitzhak Ben-Ner. During their visits to the *al-Ahram* building in Gala' Street, a few of them met Naguib Mahfouz in his small office on "the writers' floor". They naturally discussed the peace process with him, and heard him enumerate the great blessing that would emerge for the region's nations when peace finally reigned. These ideas were, and remained, permanent and unalterable components of Mahfouz's thinking.

At the end of September 1979 I finally wrote to him. My letter was dispatched via the Israeli journalist Aharon Barnea, who returned from Cairo with Mahfouz's reply – a lengthy, warm letter written on

---

10 Several years later I wrote a study of the 1975 book in which I traced the manifestations of the "new rhythm" and pointed out that in *Tales of Our Alley*, Mahfouz is using, probably for the first time in modern Arabic fiction, the narrative tense normally referred to as "historical present" (e.g., "He sees" instead of "He saw".)

October 20, 1979. The novelist reiterated his opinion of what I had written about him in my English book, and this time he added

> I thank you for your appraisal of the role I fulfilled in Arabic liter-
> ature, but I hope you have not overstated my merits. . . . Let us pray
> together that the efforts being made today will be crowned with
> success, and that our two nations will return to the fruitful path of
> coexistence, as in days of old. . . . Our two nations have known
> fruitful coexistence, in ancient times, in the Middle Ages, and in the
> modern period, while the periods of conflict and dispute have been
> few and far between. But, to my great sorrow, we have over-chron-
> icled the moments of conflict a hundred fold more than we have
> recorded long generations of friendship and partnership. I dream of
> the day when this region will be transformed through our mutual
> cooperation, [and become] a dwelling-place radiating the light of
> science, inspired by the highest divine principles. (A copy of this
> letter appears at the back of this book on page 168.)

I would have immediately packed up and left for Cairo to meet him, but entrance visas to Egypt were given primarily to diplomats and journalists, and I did not belong to either category. Only in early 1980, while I was on sabbatical in Oxford, did the long-awaited visa arrive. I caught a night flight to Cairo. The next morning I phoned Mahfouz at his home. His wife answered and upon hearing my name welcomed me warmly. Her husband had gone out for his morning stroll but would call as soon as he returned. "He's been waiting for you for quite some time", she added. I bided my time back at the hotel, and when the phone rang I heard the velvety voice of Mahfouz. A few hours later I was seated in his apartment in the Agouza quarter on the banks of the Nile. On my return to the hotel I jotted down the following:

> January 14, 1980, 6 P.M. – Visited Naguib Mahfouz at his apart-
> ment. He is thin and fragile. Extremely cordial, just as I imagined
> through all the indirect contact I had with him up till now. He and
> his wife displayed unquestionable amity. I spoke with him for two
> hours on everything under the sun; in the end he handed me a gift,
> his two latest books. . . . We didn't discuss political matters, but at
> one point I mentioned that I had always admired him for never

having lapsed into a hatred of Israel, not even during the darkest hours of the conflict. His reply was, "I have viewed the conflict as a tragedy destructive to both sides". Among other things, Mahfouz . . . expressed a great liking for a story by Agnon, of all people. This is only a first meeting (I hope).

I met him every day during my week's stay in Cairo, and the topics of our conversations expanded to include not only literary and political matters but also personal experiences. Mahfouz was especially interested in my Jewish-Arab background, my family's history in Baghdad, and the way I had mastered the Hebrew language after arriving in Israel. He would frequently ask me about the similarity between Hebrew and Arabic. During one of our discussions I inquired about the ban the Arab League had placed on his work after he made public his support of the Middle East peace process. He did not seem upset by it, but he did express anger at Arab publishers, especially in Lebanon, who had exploited the prohibition in order to churn out pirated editions of his novels. When I asked whether his burgeoning contact with Israeli critics and writers would hurt him, he calmed me though he admitted that certain Egyptian and Arab literary critics who used to write about his works were now avoiding him because of the public praise he lavished on Israeli literary scholarship. Some of them had stopped reviewing his new books altogether. But, he believed, this was only a temporary phenomenon.

During the following years I often visited Mahfouz in Cairo. The Egyptian press was vitriolic about the cordial relations evolving between the great writer (partially banned) and his Israeli guests; these attacks intensified in 1982 following the Israeli invasion of Lebanon and the brutal siege of Beirut. During one of my visits to Cairo in 1983, I invited Mahfouz to Israel to participate in a conference being held at Tel Aviv University upon the inauguration of a chair in Arabic literature. He apologized and explained that he could not visit Israel because he never traveled abroad. The day after our conversation, however, Mahfouz handed me a congratulatory letter he had written on his own initiative, and he requested that I pass it on to Professor Moshe Mani, president of my university. The letter was read during the ceremony in April 1983 and published in Israeli newspapers. His support roused angry responses in Egypt. The following comment appeared in an article published by a noted Egyptian novelist, Yusuf al-Qaʻid, in the Cairo monthly *al-Mawqif al-ʻArabi* under the title "The Israeli Enemy Does Nothing But Perpetrate Aggression and Naguib Mahfouz Does Nothing But Congratulate the Enemy!":

> We naïvely believed that Naguib Mahfouz had recovered from the Israeli disease, and we imagined that the man would now turn over a new leaf, and that we should help him inscribe the first word on this new page. However it seems that all these expectations were illusory, and the man is still gambling on the Israeli enemy, the nemesis of Egypt, the Arab world, one hundred million Arabs – yesterday's enemy, today's, and even tomorrow's.

It wasn't only Mahfouz's relations with Israelis or his undeviating support of peace that produced such wrath. Many people, especially the Nasserites, were furious with him because of his high regard for Anwar el-Sadat, as expressed in his declarations and writing, especially in his book *Facing the Throne* (1983), which appeared after Sadat's death. Here he portrayed the assassinated leader as a prince of war and a champion of peace, as opposed to Nasser, who is depicted as someone who implicated his homeland in unnecessary wars and military adventures.

Mahfouz was awarded the Nobel Prize for Literature in October 1988, at a moment of intense political and literary ostracism. I heard the announcement while I was at Princeton University in the United States. The world press received the announcement with surprise. Literary editors in U.S. newspapers went hunting for material on an Egyptian writer whom they had never heard of. Over the next few days, I gave many media interviews in the U.S. I tried to evade political questions, restricting my comments to the essence of Mahfouz's works and his tremendous contribution to modern Arabic literature. Still, one reader of Arab background wrote to the *Washington Post* complaining that even when the Arabs were finally awarded an international prize, the western media turned to an Israeli scholar! I sent my congratulations to Mahfouz, and received a reply typed on *al-*

Ahram letterhead, for the newspaper now provided him with a private secretary.

Preparations were underway in Egypt for a series of celebrations; among the invited guests were some of Mahfouz's harshest critics and detractors. On the other hand (and perhaps for the best) I was not called on to take part in any of the festivities. For months Mahfouz was caught up in the media circus that forced him to alter his quiet lifestyle. He had to appear before television cameras and journalists' flashbulbs several times a day. On my return to Israel from an extended sabbatical in the United States in December 1991, I stopped off in Egypt to celebrate his eightieth birthday, and I penned the following impression soon after:

To be near Naguib Mahfouz these days [is] a trying experience. A frail, dejected man, a veritable broken vessel. The previous month he had been flown to London, almost forcibly, to undergo open-heart surgery. The operation apparently succeeded, but the patient did not completely recover. His body appears shrunken; his voice is practically inaudible, and worst of all, his legs are too weak to support his delicate frame, which means he can no longer take his daily walks along the bustling Cairo sidewalks that he loves so much. This has been the first time that I did not hear his deep, rolling laughter . . .

In the new opera house, writers, diplomats and ambassadors gathered to mark [his birthday]. Local newspapers expressly noted that the Arab ambassadors would all participate. These are the ambassadors of countries that have boycotted and ostracized the Egyptian novelist in recent years for the sole reason that he supported peace and reconciliation with Israel.

I try to speak with him as usual about literature, but he exhibits no interest. The only subject that arouses a glint of excitement is the current peace talks between Israel and its neighbors. He fondly recalls the name of the late president, Sadat. After his death, Mahfouz said, his name began to slip somehow from the memory of the Egyptians, and it was anathema to many intellectuals who forgot that the man returned both honor and territory to his fatherland. Since the time of King Akhnaton, he adds, there has not been a leader of peace like him in Egypt, and history should remember him with veneration.

I did not ask him about his work as a novelist. That was a sensitive topic now. From the moment he was awarded the Nobel Prize for Literature in 1988, his wellspring of creativity almost completely dried up. His last work, A False Dawn, which appeared two years ago, included nearly twenty marvelous stories, crystal-clear and brimming with literary vigor, but all of them were written prior to 1988. The prize has forced the entire Arab world to recognize him as its greatest national writer; but the Arab League's ban of his works had deprived him of his joie de vivre.

The fact that during the following years his works have been translated and published by some of the world's best publishing houses has left him, so it appeared, apathetic. Likewise, the scores of articles written about him all over the world do not attract his interest. On no account is this due to conceit or contempt, but because the urge to write, or the capability, has deserted him.

Suddenly, at the end of 1988, the literary boycott had been lifted, and hundreds of writers, journalists, and public figures throughout the entire Arab world made a pilgrimage to Cairo to express their friendship and admiration. Mahfouz did not remind his past detractors about the ban they had placed on him, nor did he demand any apologies. However, after several years, he was able to score a point when, in September 1996, the Jordanian writer and general secretary of the Arab Writers Association, Fakhri Qa'war, visited him in his office in the *al-Ahram* building. Qa'war had been among the most radical defamers of "renegades", and numerous boycotts of other Arab writers could be chalked up to his "credit". Leading the list was the great Syrian poet, Adonis, who had been expelled from membership in the Arab Writers Association because he had once met with Israeli writers and public officials. Qa'war asked Mahfouz, according to the *al-Ahram* reporter, if he was familiar with of the Arab Writers Association. Mahfouz spontaneously burst out, laughing, "And how should I not be familiar with the association? I was expelled from its membership!"

On Friday, September 14, 1994, Mahfouz, aged 83, was brutally assaulted outside his house in Agouza by a Muslim fanatic, incited by men who wanted to punish Mahfouz for views they believed were contradictory to the essence of Islam. The attack came as a delayed response to his novel *Children of Our Alley*, which was published, it will be recalled, in serial form in *al-Ahram* at the end of 1959 – in other words, thirty-five years prior to the assault. Although the Nobel Prize freed him from the venomous pens of those who opposed the peace process and despised Sadat, it nevertheless generated hysterical salvos from leading Islamic fundamentalists in his country. The Nobel Prize Committee had mentioned this forbidden novel in its rationale for granting him the award, which again brought the writer into the headlines and generated hundreds of hostile articles and several hate books against him. The blind sheikh Omar Abdul al-Rahman, one of the most fanatic leaders of Egyptian fundamentalists and the mastermind behind the explosion in the World Trade Center in New York in 1993, had been seeking Mahfouz's blood since 1989. He even claimed that had he moved against him immediately after publication of the novel in 1959, Salman Rushdie (who was also "sentenced" to death for his literary work) would never have dared to write his *Satanic Verses*.

Mahfouz survived the assassin's attack, but his health was ravaged from a severe wound in his neck, and the nerves in his right arm and hand were so badly hurt that he lost the ability to hold a pen. He ceased writing altogether and refused to either dictate his thoughts or try adjusting to a custom-made computer. (Until the attempt on his life, he wrote a weekly column in *al-Ahram*.) He repeatedly explained to his friends that for seventy years he had worked by gripping a pen between his fingers, that was how he had written all his books, and he could not change his habits at such an advanced age.

I did not see Mahfouz during the long months of recuperation and was able to visit him only a year later. He was quiet and withdrawn, although he would occasionally surprise me with the sudden reappearance of his old vivacity. As I held his swollen right hand, my wife ventured to ask him what I had not dared to. Does he not feel the urge to write? For a second, I thought that he did not hear the question, but after a brief silence he answered in a steady voice, "No, the desire to write comes to me the moment I sit at a table and hold a pen. That condition, however, no longer exists".

Between 1995 and 1998 I lived in Cairo and served as director of the Israel Academic Center in that city. Founded in 1982, the center had been a topic of our conversations during the 1980s, and Mahfouz expressed support for its goal of nurturing cooperation between the Egyptian and Israeli academic communities. He was unhappy about articles in the Egyptian press charging that the center was the vanguard of a "cultural invasion" or an offshoot of the Israeli intelligence services. He had willingly met with all of its previous heads and encouraged Egyptian writers to visit its premises; but he himself refrained from actively participating in its events. Once, though, he had promised that he would come if and when I became its director. But now, in 1995, I did not dare invite him. Since the assassination attempt, he had ceased going to "unsafe" places. He was not free to choose where he could visit; he was constantly accompanied by an armed bodyguard (for fear of another attempt on his life). Every time he went out, he was chauffeured from his home and back by one of his close friends. Even the telephone was not a useful means of communicating with him because of his poor hearing. In my first year in Cairo, I did not even try to meet him for fear that a stray journalist might spot us together and report it, providing ammunition for fanatics and malcontents. However, in the middle of 1996, a mutual friend told me that the novelist frequently asked about me, and would like to see me. I began visiting Mahfouz at places not patronized by journalists, for example the Sofitel Hotel, where he would come on occasion to meet his friends at a designated hour in the evening. In this manner we renewed our friendship.

He would sit among his companions talking and joking although he could not hear everything being said. Occasionally he would interrupt a conversation, add something, and to our great surprise his responses were always on target, even if it was obvious that many details of the conversation had eluded him. When I tried to address him he did not always hear me, at which point an Egyptian colleague would intervene and "translate" my words in a louder voice. When we were left alone or in the presence of a close friend, he would start to reminisce about the years he was free to wander the sidewalks and sit in outdoor cafés on Tal'at Harb Street or on the banks of the Nile. He would recall mutual friends of ours who had passed away, such as the Israeli ex-general, Arabic scholar, and peace activist Matti Peled, who wrote about Mahfouz's works and knew him personally. He would also remember with much grief the Alexandrene Coptic novelist Na'im Takla, whose untimely death after a long illness occurred in 1996; and above all he would lovingly remember a great friend of both of us, the late Dr. Husayn Fawzi, who died in 1988.

Toward the end of my term at the Center, in July 1998, I made a farewell visit to the Sofitel. This time two Israeli friends, Ronit Matalon and Sami Michael, accompanied me. Michael, a prominent Israeli novelist, had translated Mahfouz's *Trilogy* into Hebrew. Mahfouz had wanted to read one of Michael's novels, but only a few pages existed in Arabic translation. In 1995 an Arabic version of Michael's novel *Victoria* appeared in Cairo, but by then it was too late. Mahfouz was unable to read it because of his weakened eyesight. At most, he would find time in the morning to listen to one of his friends read newspaper selections.

This was Matalon's first meeting with Mahfouz. Born in Israel, her family hailed from Egypt, and her novels and short stories often reflected her Egyptian background. She was obviously very excited throughout the evening, especially as Mahfouz had received her with visible warmth. Before long Ronit lost her somewhat tense look, and we all fell into a friendly discussion, with Mahfouz's laughter enlivening the atmosphere and dissipating the gloom that had engulfed him earlier that evening. Toward eight o'clock our good friend 'Ali Salem, a well-known Egyptian playwright, arrived and reminded us that the final game of the World Soccer Cup would begin very shortly; he invited us, the Israelis, to watch the game with him on a large screen in a downtown hotel. I caught a glimpse of the face of Mahfouz's bodyguard, pleading that we wind up our meeting so that he too could watch the game. The writer Naim Sabri, Mahfouz's escort that evening, announced that he had to drive Mahfouz home and would catch up with us later at the hotel. We got the message and bid Naguib Mahfouz farewell.

In December 2001 Naguib Mahfouz reached the age of 90. I had accompanied his oeuvre for over three decades, and had had the honor of spending many hours in his company. During this period he himself was introduced to Israeli reality (albeit from a distance) and had met quite a few Israelis. Unlike Egyptian intellectuals of the younger generation, he encouraged visitors from Israel to meet with him, and did not try to conceal his connections with them.

I recall once, at the beginning of the summer of 1982, that I arrived in Cairo on a Wednesday, and the following morning made my way to the *al-Ahram* building, as was my custom, without arranging a meeting in advance, since I knew that this was Mahfouz's regular *al-Ahram* day. As I approached the fifth floor I heard young voices, and in the writer's small room I found a group of Israeli students from Ben-Gurion University, sporting sandals and typical Israeli summer attire. They sat crowded on the floor of the room and asked their host questions about his work, in particular about the content of his novels that had been translated into Hebrew. When I entered the room, I heard him trying to convince his young audience that the writer should not serve as an interpreter of his own works. The work of the writer ends when he sends his book to print. From that moment the work becomes common property, and any reader has the right to interpret it as he sees fit. In those same days anti-normalization voices and those wary of Israel's "cultural invasion" began to be heard from within the Egyptian intellectual community. I was therefore surprised at Mahfouz's daring in openly inviting a group of Israeli students to the home of *al-Ahram*, which had been established and cultivated by Muhammad Hasanein Haykal, one of Nasserism's chief spokesmen. This meeting struck me as a tangible expression of normalization and as the beginning of true cultural dialogue.

Since then, however, the voices of opposition and rejection of such dialogue have grown. The writer himself confided in me at the end of his meeting with the students, that it was not the literary discussion that motivated him to give of his time to the Israeli group, but rather his desire to meet young people who had grown up in an atmosphere of a long and protracted bloody conflict, and for whom a horizon for peace had opened. It is our duty, he added, to nurture the culture of peace on both sides of the border. In the meantime, it is difficult to say that a great wind is coming, or that Mahfouz's fantastic dream about the day when our region will turn into a great house of cooperation and creativity has been realized. Yet nonetheless, and despite it all, the peace has endured!

Mahfouz's death at 95 in August 2006 marked the end of a moving chapter in my personal and academic life. I was with him when several of his later books appeared, and I felt fortunate to be able to introduce his literary works to a readership that could not read his books in their original. And above all, his friendship and unwavering principles were road signs that accompanied me for more than three decades.

1 With Naguib Mahfouz in his latter years, Cairo, 2004.

2 The author with his family, Ramat Gan, Israel, 1996.

3 Avigal, the author's daughter, with Naguib Mahfouz at the novelist's residence, Cairo, 1982.

4 Professsor Haim Blanc listening to recordings of Arabic dialects, *c.* 1960.

5 Professor S. D. Goitein, *c.* 1980.

6 Dr. Mustafa Badawi at his office, Pusey Lane, Oxford, c. 1990.

7 Dr. Husayn Fawzi with Terrie Somekh, Paris, 1980.

8 With Egyptian writer Naim Takla (*right*) and Israeli writer Aharon Amir (*left*), Alexandria, 1990.

9 With Egyptian playwright Ali Salem at the Israeli Academic Center, Cairo, 1996.

10 With Naguib Mahfouz at Champs Elysees Café, Alexandria, 1982.

11 With Professor Edward Said, Stockholm, 1993.

Opposite page
12 With Mrs. Shulamit Aloni, former Israeli minister of education and Professor Ali Atiyya, professor of Hebrew literature at Eyn Shams University, Cairo. Photo taken in Tel Aviv, *c.* 1997.

13 At the Israeli Academic Center in Cairo during a lecture by Israeli novelist Sami Michael (third from left), 1995.

الأستاذ ساسون سوميخ

اليه صادق تحياتي وشكري وبعد

فقد اطلعت على رسالتك بسرور صادق ، اعترف لك عما أنه لك مني شكر لعنايتك بتلك الأدبية بدراسة أدبي ، وقد صدمتني أكثر من مجال بأبه كتابك عني يعتبر عملا نقديا عميقا وشاملا ، وانه يقترب من أفضل ما كتب عني من ما كتب أفضلك جميعا . وطبيعي اني لست فيه منك من أدب العرب ولاحظت أني لم تجر بأي من عقلية عدو . بل اسر دراستك كانت فنية في المقام الأول وانسانية بالمعنى الشامل والقديم .

واني أوافقك مع الأسباب التي منعتك من الاتصال بي وانت بصدد التأليف والبعد عن الاتصال بالمؤلف ـ مبدأ عام يجري به بعض العلماء ذات الموضوعية ، ان يتخذ الحصول عليك ـ فيرى أنه ليس بأي حال مفضل ، ونميل لأكتب المعبر عن الصدق في محاضرة جلسة يبلغك للغير يقدم ما تأتب لاكتشاف ضفه الأهداف وبالتالي لكتشاف انفسنا واكتشاف بهم ، أود لك هذا الغالب في علم ثم ابراج العمر . شكرا لك تقديرك لدرمي في يوم قريب ان شاء الله . ولنضع الله عما كلا ارجو ان اشاركك بنفسي في يوم قريب ان شاء الله ، وان يعود شجاعا الى العاشرة ابتكامل الملامس المبذولة اليوم بالنجاح الثمرة كما كان ذلك في منظ المعدل . فما لاشك فيه اننا تعاونا تمر قام به من سجينا عن مدى الأعظم الدولة في المعهد العدني والوسط والحديث ، وان أيام الدفاع م كانت قصيرة وقليلة " غير اننا وبالأسف هنينا بتسجيل لحظات الدفاع م الى ما شاء مرة مستجيل اجيال الصداقة والتعاون ، واني اعلم بعد يميل بنفس التقارب المشترك هذه المنطقة لا مقام رفيع مثل على العلم مبارك جهادك السيم السامية .

والى اللقاء يا سيدي الأستاذ العزيز وانت واوطاننا في خيرحال

المخلص

نجيب محفوظ

القاهرة   ١٩٧٨/١٠/١٢

A letter dated October 12, 1978, sent from Cairo by Egyptian novelist Naguib Mahfouz to the author in Tel Aviv, in which he confirms reading the latter's book The Changing Rhythm (1973).